If Only They Could Talk

A vet's life is never just a peaceful rest in the country, as James Herriot will tell you.

The phone rings in the middle of the night, ten large pigs escape and run riot in the market place, a cow needs a piece of wire removed from its stomach and an old lady's dog suffers from eating too much.

The young vet learns to cope with the animals and, hardest of all, their owners. The stories he tells are sometimes sad but mostly very funny indeed.

The BULLS-EYE series

General Editor   PATRICK NOBES

If Only They Could Talk

Adapted by Jean Nobes
from *If Only They Could Talk*
by James Herriot

Hutchinson

London Sydney Auckland Johannesburg

Hutchinson Education

An imprint of Century Hutchinson Ltd
62–65 Chandos Place, London WC2N 4NW

Century Hutchinson Australia Pty Ltd
89–91 Albion Street, Surry Hills,
New South Wales 2010, Australia

Century Hutchinson New Zealand Limited
PO Box 40-086, Glenfield, Auckland 10,
New Zealand

Century Hutchinson South Africa (Pty) Ltd
PO Box 337, Bergvlei 2012, South Africa

Original novel first published by Michael Joseph 1970
© James Herriot 1970

This adaptation first published 1979
Reprinted 1981, 1982, 1983, 1988 (twice)

© This adaptation Jean Nobes 1979

Set in Monotype Baskerville

Printed and bound in Great Britain by
The Guernsey Press Co. Ltd, Guernsey, Channel Islands

British Library Cataloguing in Publication Data
Nobes, Jean
    If only they could talk.—(Bulls-eye book).
    1. Readers — Veterinary medicine
    I. Herriot, James. If only they could talk.
    Adaptations III. Series
    428'.6'2   PE1126.D4

ISBN 0 09 140391 X

Contents

1 My welcome

It was hot in the little bus. I was on the wrong side where the hot sun beat on the windows. I had my best suit on and a stiff white collar. It was a silly outfit for July, but I was on my way to try to get a job, so I had to look smart. I had just passed my exams to be a vet. Jobs were hard to get in 1937 and a lot of new vets like me were on the dole. I could hardly believe my luck when the letter came. It said that Mr Siegfried Farnon MRCVS would like to see me on Friday afternoon. I was to have tea with him, and stay the night at his house. If he liked me I would get the job. I had almost given up hope of getting a job, as so many of my friends were out of work.

I had never been to Yorkshire before. I looked out of the bus window in surprise. Instead of the mills and factories I expected to see, I saw high grassy hills and wide valleys. There were no fences, only dry-stone walls at the edge of the road. They went round the fields and up on to the green hills.

As I sat thinking about Siegfried Farnon I suddenly found the bus had stopped. We were in a square in the middle of a small grey town.

Darrowby did not get much space in the guide books. All they said was that it was a little town on a river, with a market place and two bridges. But when you looked at it you saw how beautiful it was. The grey stone houses stood close to the bright river, and above them were the high slopes of the fells.

The air was so clear, already the dirt and grime and smoke of the city seemed far away. Now I was here, right on the doorstep of Skeldale House where Siegfried Farnon lived. I liked the look of the old house. Ivy climbed up the bricks. It had no front garden, and the front door opened right on to the street.

I rang the bell and suddenly the quiet was broken by a sound like a wolf pack in full cry. I peeped through the glass door and saw a river of dogs coming towards me. If I had not been used to dogs I would have run for my life. After a minute or two I was able to count the dogs. In fact there were five of them, not a dozen as I first thought.

I was thinking of ringing the bell again when I saw a big woman coming to open the door. She shouted one word to the dogs and the noise stopped as if by magic. When she opened the door I said with my best smile:

'Good afternoon. My name is James Herriot. Mr Farnon is expecting me. He wrote and asked me to come today.'

'Mr Herriot?' she said. 'Surgery is from six to seven o'clock.'

'No, no,' I said. 'I've come to try to get a job as his assistant.'

'Assistant? Well, that's nice,' she said. 'I'm Mrs Hall. I keep house for Mr Farnon. He's not married, you know. He never said anything to me about you. Never mind. Come in and have a cup of tea.'

She led me through the house to the back, and into a sunny room. It looked out on to a big, untidy garden. In the room was an old worn carpet, and plain furniture. To my surprise I saw on the shelf over the fire a pint pot. It was stuffed full of bank notes and cheques. I was looking at this when Mrs Hall came in with a tray of tea.

'I suppose Mr Farnon is out on a case,' I said.

'No. He's gone to visit his mother. I can't say when he'll be back,' said Mrs Hall and left me to my tea.

The dogs were quiet. They came and sat around the room. Soon they fell asleep. But I could not relax with them. I felt let down. This was all very odd. Why should Siegfried Farnon write for an assistant, fix a time to meet him, then go and visit his mother? Another thing – the housekeeper had never heard of me. She had not been told to get a room ready for me, it seemed.

As I sat thinking the door bell rang. The dogs, as if touched by a live wire, shot into the air. They threw themselves through the door, barking and screaming. There was no sign of Mrs Hall, so I went to the front door. There the dogs were barking at the tops of their voices.

'Shut up!' I yelled, and the din stopped. The five dogs looked very sad. I opened the door.

A fat man with a round face stood there.

'Hello, hello, Mr Farnon in?' he asked.

'Not at the moment. Can I help you?' I asked.

'Give him a message when he comes in,' he said. 'Tell him Bert Sharpe has a cow that wants boring out.'

'Boring out?' I asked.

9

'That's right. She's only going on three cylinders,' he said.

'Three cylinders?' I asked.

'Yes, and if we don't do something, she'll go wrong in her udder, won't she?' he said.

'Of course,' I said.

'Don't want felon, do we? You tell him then. Goodbye.'

I went back into the sitting-room. I had listened to my first case-history, and not understood a word of it.

The bell rang again. This time I shouted before the dogs began to bark, so they stayed where they were. It was a man with a cloth cap on his head.

He took out his clay pipe and said: 'My name is Mulligan. I want Mr Farnon to make up some medicine for my dog.'

'What's the trouble with your dog?' I asked.

He put his hand to his ear and looked puzzled. He must be deaf, I thought. I asked him again loudly what the trouble was.

'He's being sick all over the place,' he said.

I felt on firm ground with this.

'How long after eating is he sick?' I asked – twice.

I thought he understood me the second time I asked him. However, all he said was, 'Oh, yes, he's being very sick, sir.'

I didn't feel like trying again, so I told him I would see to it for him later. He must have been able to read my lips. He smiled and walked away. Back in the sitting-room I sank into a chair and poured a cup of tea. I leaned back and closed my eyes. I went over in my mind the strange things that had happened to me since I had arrived in Darrowby.

2 Siegfried Farnon

I opened my eyes. Somebody was saying 'hello'. A tall thin man tood in front of me, his hands in his pockets. As I got to my feet he held out his hand and said, 'Sorry you've had to wait. I'm Siegfried Farnon.'

He looked as if he didn't spend much time in front of a mirror. He had a small moustache, and untidy sandy hair. He was wearing an old tweed jacket. The collar of his shirt was worn out. He gave me a long look after we had greeted each other. Then he said, 'Come on. I want to show you round the place.'

Farnon went to the first of the doors that led off the passage. He opened the door and said very proudly, 'This is the dispensary – where the medicines are kept.'

The dispensary was an important place to a vet in the days before all the new drugs came ready mixed from the drug firms. I knew all the names on the bottles on the shelves. They had been part of my training. These shelves held all the weapons vets had in those days against animal sickness.

The two of us stood looking at the rows of bottles. We had no idea then that most of them were of no use. We did not know that the days of the old medicines were nearly over. Soon they would be forgotten.

'This is where we keep the instruments,' said Siegfried, as he showed me into another little room. The small animal instruments lay on shelves, very neat and clean. The large animal instruments hung on the walls, from hooks.

We finished up in the operating room. It had bare white walls, a high table, and an oxygen and gas outfit.

'Not much small animal work here,' said Siegfried. 'But when there is, it makes a nice change from lying on your belly in a cow shed '

We went out into the passage. He asked, 'Well, what do you think of it all?'

'Great,' I said. 'You've got just about everything you need here.' He looked pleased.

Back in the sitting-room I told him about Bert Sharpe. 'He said something about boring out a cow which was going on three cylinders. He talked about felon. I didn't understand.'

Siegfried laughed. 'He means that his cow has a blocked teat. Felon is the local word for swelling of the udder.'

'Well, thanks. Then there was a deaf Irishman, a Mr Mulligan. . . .'

'I know,' said Siegfried. 'Is his dog being sick?'

'Yes,' I said.

'Right, I'll put up some medicine for him. I like to treat that dog at a distance. It's as big as a donkey. It's had Joe Mulligan on the ground a few times. Just gets him down and worries him when it's got nothing better to do. But Joe loves it.'

'Why is it being sick?' I asked.

'That doesn't mean a thing,' said Siegfried. 'It eats

every bit of rubbish it finds. Well, we had better get out to Bert Sharpe's. And there are one or two other visits. How about coming with me and I'll show you a bit of the country around here?'

So off we went.

3 Out on the job

Outside the house stood Siegfried's car. As I moved towards it I saw that it was in a bad way. The tyres were bald, the bodywork rusty, and the windscreen cracked. However, I did not see that the passenger seat was not fixed to the floor. I got into the car, sat in the seat and went over backwards. I ended up with my head on the back seat and my feet against the roof. Siegfried said he was sorry, helped me up, and we set off.

Siegfried was a strange driver. He was so overcome by the beauty of the view, that he drove slowly down the hill out of the town. He rested his elbows on the wheel and cupped his chin in his hands. At the bottom of the hill he came out of his dream and began to drive at seventy miles an hour. The old car rocked madly. My seat moved from side to side as I jammed my feet against the floor.

Suddenly he put the brakes full on and pointed out some beautiful cows in a field. Off we went again. He never looked at the road in front. He spent a lot of time driving fast, and looking around him at the same time.

We left the road at last and made our way up a lane. We stopped in a farmyard and Siegfried said, 'There is a lame horse here.' The farmer led out a big cart horse for us to see.

Siegfried asked: 'Like to have a look at it?'

I put my hand on the lame foot. It felt hot. 'Looks like pus in the foot to me,' I said.

'I'll bet you're right,' said Siegfried. 'You'd better open it up. I'll watch you.'

I knew that he was testing me. I took the knife, lifted the foot and held it between my knees. I had to find the dark mark on the sole where the germs had got in. Then I had to cut at it till I reached the pus. I found the dark spot and started to cut.

The hoof seemed hard as iron. The horse seemed to like having its sore foot lifted off the ground. He put all his weight on my back. I groaned and dug him in the ribs, but he still leaned on me.

The sweat was in my eyes and my back felt as if it would soon break. I wanted a rest, but with Siegfried's eyes on me I couldn't take one. I cut away at the hoof and my knees began to shake. The horse rested happily on me. I wondered how things would look when I fell flat on my face. At last a thin stream of pus came out of the hoof.

The farmer looked pleased. It took me a long time to stand up straight. I could feel my shirt sticking to my back. I stood back from the horse.

'Well done, Herriot,' said Siegfried. 'It isn't funny when the hoof is as hard as that.'

We did two more visits. First we went to a calf with a cut leg which I stitched. Then we went to see Bert Sharpe's cow with a blocked teat. He led us to the cow shed.

'See what you can make of that,' said Siegfried. I got

down and felt the teat. I could feel a thick mass half way up. I began to push a thin metal instrument up the teat. One second later I was sitting in the dung, where the cow had kicked me. There was nothing I could do but sit there fighting for breath, my mouth open like a fish.

I took my time to get over the kick, then I stood up. While Mr Sharpe held the nose and Siegfried lifted the tail, I moved the blockage.

When it was over the farmer smiled and said, 'Great! She's going on four cylinders now!'

4 A visit to the pub

We took a steep winding way home. We climbed higher and still higher. The hill-side fell away suddenly to a dark valley. A rocky stream rushed down to the country below. On the top, we got out of the car.

I looked around. Siegfried turned towards me and said, 'This is one of the wildest places in England. An awful place in winter. I've known this pass to be blocked with snow for weeks on end. But isn't it beautiful?'

It was dark when we got back into the car and started the long drive down into the valley. We came to a silent village and Siegfried put the brakes on. I shot across the floor and banged into the windscreen.

'There's a grand little pub here,' said Siegfried. 'Let's go in and have a beer.'

This sort of pub was something new to me. It was a big square kitchen. A huge fireplace and an old black cooking range took up one end. About a dozen men sat around, backs to the walls. In front of them, rows of pint mugs rested on the oak tables.

It was quiet when we went in. Then someone said hello to us. They were mostly farmers or farm workers out to enjoy their evening. Most of them were burnt red by the sun. Some were playing dominoes in the corner.

Siegfried and I sat down. He got two beers for us.

'Well, you can have the job if you want it,' he said to me. 'Four quid a week and full board. OK?'

I was in! And four pounds a week! That was real money in those days.

'Thank you,' I said. 'I'll take the job.'

'Good,' Siegfried said. 'Let me tell you more about it.' And he told me about the sort of things he wanted me to do, what the local people were like and what his plans were. The beer kept coming, and the pub grew hotter and hotter. More people came in and the noise grew. Soon I felt I had known everyone for years. I had a lovely time.

Then it was time to go. Out we went into the dark village street with our new friends. A young man opened the car door for me. I got in as I waved good-bye. This time the seat went over faster than usual. I fell backwards and came to rest with my head among some boots and my knees tucked under my chin.

A row of surprised faces looked at me through the back window. But soon hands helped me up, and the trick seat was put up again. As we drove home I wondered how long it had been like that, and if Siegfried had thought of having it fixed.

5 A bad start

The next day I had my first chance to work alone. The past five years had led up to this one moment. Siegfried had gone off to visit his mother again. What a loving son, I thought. He had said he would be back late, so I was in charge.

I didn't have long to wait before the telephone rang.

'Is that Mr Farnon?' asked a deep voice.

'No, I'm sorry, he's out. This is his assistant,' I said.

The voice asked, 'When will he be back?'

'Not till late, I'm afraid. Can I do anything for you?'

'I don't know. I am Mr Soames, Lord Hulton's farm manager. I have a valuable hunting horse with colic. Do you know anything about colic?'

This made me angry, but all I said was, 'I'm a vet, so I should know something about it.'

There was a long silence, then the voice said, 'Well, you'll have to do. In any case, I know the medicine the horse wants. And for God's sake don't take all night getting here. How long will you be?'

'I'm on my way,' I said.

'Right.' He rang off. My face felt hot. So my first case wasn't going to be easy. Colics were tricky, and Soames sounded nasty. As I drove the eight miles to the farm, I wondered what I'd find at the end of the journey.

A man stood waiting for me in the farmyard. He stood with his back towards me, and did not turn as I came up to him.

'Mr Soames?' I asked.

At first he did not move, then he turned very slowly. He had a thick red neck, a ruddy face, and small angry eyes.

'Yes, I'm Mr Soames.' He stressed the 'Mr' as though it meant a lot to him. 'I'm a very great friend of Mr Farnon,' he said.

'I think you have a horse with colic,' I said. I wished my voice didn't sound so high.

'In there' he said, pointing to one of the horse-boxes. 'One of Lord Hulton's best hunters.'

I opened the door and went in. I was shocked by what I saw. It was a very large box. The floor was covered in moss. A bay horse staggered round the edge of the box. He had worn a deep path in the moss. He was covered in sweat from nose to tail. His nostrils were wide and his eyes stared in front of him. His head rolled about at every step. Through his teeth drops of foam fell to the floor from his mouth.

My mouth had gone dry. I could hardly speak.

'How long has he been like this?' I asked.

'Oh, he had a bit of pain in his belly this morning. I've been giving him medicine all day, at least this fellow has,' said Soames.

I saw that a big fat man stood in the corner of the box.

'It would take more than stomach medicine to help him,' I said. 'This is not colic.'

'What the hell is it then?' asked Soames.

'Well, I can't say till I've examined him, but he's in such awful pain it looks like a twisted bowel,' I said.

He laughed and said, 'Twisted bowel my foot! He's got a bit of pain in his belly, that's all. What are you going to do?'

I turned to the big man in the corner, and asked him to put a head collar on the horse so I could examine him.

When they put the collar on the horse, he stood still. He shook and groaned as I took his pulse. It was as bad as it could be. He had a temperature of 103°.

I asked the big man to get me a bucket of hot water, soap and a towel so that I could wash. I wanted to examine the horse's bowel.

When the water came I soaped my arm and put it into the horse's rectum. I could feel that the bowel was twisted. As I touched it the horse shuddered in pain.

What was I to do? What could I say? I took a deep breath and told Soames what I thought.

'All right, have it your own way. Only for God's sake do something,' he said.

'There's nothing anybody can do. There's no cure for this. All I can do is put him out of pain,' I said.

Soames looked at me, amazed, and said, 'What do you mean?'

'I mean that I should shoot him now. He has been going through hell all day. He's dying now, and he's in dreadful pain,' I replied.

Soames sank his head in his hands. 'Oh God, why did this have to happen? His lordship is on holiday or I'd call him out to talk some sense into you. Look here, can't we wait till Mr Farnon gets back?'

I thought how easy it would be to wait for Siegfried to decide about the horse. I looked again at the horse, as he stumbled round and round the box, trying to leave the pain behind. He lifted his head and gave a little groan. It was a cry for help, and I knew what to do.

I went out and got the humane killer from the car. 'Steady his head,' I said to the big man, and put the killer to the horse's head, between his eyes. There was a sharp crack, and the horse fell to the ground.

Soames stared at the horse as if he could not believe his eyes. I told him that Mr Farnon would be round in the morning to see if he agreed with my opinion.

I put on my jacket and went out to the car. As I started up, Soames opened the door and put his head in.

'I'm going to tell his lordship about this, and Mr Farnon too,' he said. 'I'll let him know what kind of assistant he's landed himself with.' He banged the door shut and walked away.

6 Siegfried steps in

Back at the surgery I sat and waited for my boss. I tried not to think that I might have lost my job. Yet I knew I couldn't have done anything else.

It was one in the morning before Siegfried came in. He did not say anything as I told him about the horse. He was about to speak when the phone rang.

'Oh, it's you Mr Soames,' Siegfried said. He was a long time saying 'Yes' and 'No' and 'I see'. Then he began to speak.

'Thank you for ringing, Mr Soames. It seems to me that Mr Herriot did the only thing he could do. It would have been cruel to leave the horse. Well, I'm sorry you feel like that, but I think my assistant is a very good vet. If I had been there I would have done the same thing. Good night, Mr Soames. I'll see you in the morning.'

I thanked Siegfried. He got us each a large whisky and sat down in the arm chair. He smiled at me and said, 'Well, you really got chucked in at the deep end tonight!'

'Soames says he's a friend of yours,' I said. 'Do you know him well?'

'Oh, I know all about him,' replied Siegfried. 'A nasty bit of work. He's no friend of mine, believe me.'

I felt much better and said, 'I wouldn't like too many nights like tonight.'

Siegfried replied, 'You never know what's in store for you in this job. One thing, you never get bored. Here, have some more whisky.'

I drank the whisky and we talked and talked. It seemed no time at all before Siegfried said, 'Well, five o'clock. Who would have thought it? But I'm glad we had a drink together. What a first case to have!'

Two and a half hours' sleep was not much of a night's sleep, but I was up by 7.30 and down for breakfast by 8 o'clock.

Even so, Siegfried had already left to examine the dead horse. I was just eating the last of the toast, when Siegfried came back.

He looked very pleased and said,

'Any coffee left? Good. I'll have a cup. Well, you've nothing to worry about. You were dead right about the twisted bowel. I'm glad you put the poor animal down right away.'

'Did you see Soames?' I asked.

'Oh, he was there, of course. He tried to get a few digs in about you, but I didn't listen. I just pointed out how angry Lord Hulton will be when he hears how his horse suffered.'

This news made me feel much better. I went over to the desk and got the day book out.

'Here are this morning's calls. What would you like me to do?' I asked.

Siegfried picked out a round of visits for me. 'Here you are,' he said. 'A few nice cases to run you in.'

Things were looking up, I thought, as I turned to go.

7 Tristan arrives

As I opened the front door, Siegfried called, 'Oh, there's one thing I'd like you to do. My young brother is hitching a lift from University today. He's training to be a vet there, and the term ends today. When he gets close, he'll give us a ring. Will you slip out and give him a lift?' I said I would, and Siegfried went on to tell me that his brother's name was Tristan. What names, I thought, Siegfried and Tristan.

In the late afternoon Tristan rang. He sounded very much like his older brother, I thought, as he told me where he was.

In spite of his voice, Tristan didn't look a bit like Siegfried. He was a short young man, with the face of a boy. His hair was dark and his smile was charming.

'Did you have much walking to do?' I asked.

He said, 'A fair bit, but it did me good. We had a wild end of term party last night.' He opened the car door and threw his rucksack in the back. As I started up, he lit a cigarette and began to read the *Daily Mirror*.

'Are your exams over now?' I asked. When he said yes I nearly asked him how he had got on, but I did not. Sometimes it's not wise. In any case, we were not short of things to talk about. Listening to him, I thought what a clever young man he seemed.

Siegfried was out when we got home. He came home in the evening, and he and I began to chat happily about work. Then Tristan came in. At once I felt less easy. Siegfried seemed to change, and Tristan's face went deadpan and his eyes looked wary. Siegfried said quietly: 'Well, how did the exams go?'

Tristan took a deep breath and told his brother that he had failed one of his exams. At first Siegfried did not speak, and the silence in the room was hard to bear.

Then suddenly he burst out, 'I think this is awful! It's a damned disgrace, that's what it is. What the hell have you been doing all this term anyway? Drinking, I should think, chasing women, spending my money, anything but work. And now you've got the bloody nerve to walk in here and tell me you've failed. You're lazy, that's your trouble, isn't it? You're bone idle!'

I hardly knew Siegfried. His face was black with rage, and his eyes glared.

He shouted wildly at Tristan: 'But I've had enough this time. I'm sick of you. I'm not going to work my fingers to the bone to keep you. This is the end. You're sacked. So get out of here. I don't want to see you around any more. Go on – get out.'

Tristan left the room. I felt dreadful. I didn't know what to say or where to look. I was so upset at what had happened. I was glad when Siegfried sent me on a call and I was able to get out of the room.

It was nearly dark when I got back. In the gloom I met Tristan at the back door, looking out at the garden. I felt I had to say something.

'Sorry about the way things turned out,' I said.

He took a pull at his cigarette, and said, 'That's all right. It could have been worse.'

I asked him what he was going to do as he had been kicked out.

'I can see you don't understand,' Tristan said. 'You needn't worry. Siegfried will have forgotten all about it in the morning.'

'Are you sure?' I asked, amazed.

'Dead sure. He's always sacking me and he always forgets. Don't worry. I'll pass my exams next time,' he said. And he smiled his charming smile.

8 Getting used to the life

Tristan had been with us for three weeks. Things had not gone too badly between the two brothers after the first row. However, Tristan did make Siegfried very angry about the night phone calls.

Siegfried had said that Tristan must answer the phone when it rang at night. Tristan was not much good at this. It usually ended up that poor Siegfried took the calls, standing in the cold passage, shivering in the dawn. Then he would race into Tristan's room, where Tristan was snug between the blankets.

'Why didn't you answer the phone like I told you? Don't tell me you're deaf as well as idle! Come on, out of it, out, out, out!' he would shout.

It all made the house feel rather tense. I was glad when I was able to get my things ready for the morning round, and escape.

At this time life was full. There were so many things to find out, and a lot I had to prove to myself. I had come to Darrowby at a bad time for me. The farmers, after a long time without a vet, had welcomed Siegfried with open arms. He was able, willing to work hard, and charming. Now I had to push my way into the act. I just was not wanted.

I was used to the questions. 'Where's the vet?' 'Is

he ill or something?' 'I wanted to see your boss.' It was sad to see their faces fall when I walked on to their farms.

But I had to admit they were fair. They would begin to warm to me when I took off my coat and showed them what I could do. And they knew how to treat visitors. 'Come in and have a bit of dinner', was something I heard nearly every day. Sometimes I was glad to say yes, and I ate some meals with them I shall not forget.

Often too, they would slip half a dozen eggs or a pound of butter into the car as I was going. I began to learn a lot about the farmers, and I liked what I found. They were tough, and they knew how to take life. If things went wrong, they shrugged them off and said, 'Well, these things happen.'

It looked like another hot day as I wound the car window down as far as it would go. I was on my way to do a TB test on a herd of cows. And this was no ordinary herd. Siegfried had told me that they were really tough. They had never been tied up. They lived out on the fells. It was not often that anybody went near them, so they were nearly wild. He said the best thing to do would be to get the farmer's two sons, Frank and George, to give me a hand, as they were used to the herd.

There were about eighty of the cattle. They had been caught and put into all the farm buildings possible. I looked at the black wild animals and they looked back at me. Their red eyes glinted from under the rough hair which fell over their faces. They swished their tails in bad temper. It was not going to be easy to give each cow an injection.

I turned to Frank and said, 'Can you get hold of these beggars for me?'

'We'll have a bloody good try,' he replied calmly.

He and his brother lit cigarettes before getting into the pens where the animals were packed. I followed them. The cattle were as bad as they looked. If I went at them from the front they came at me with their great hairy heads. If I went behind, they kicked at me.

But the brothers amazed me. One of them would drop a halter on the beast. He would get his fingers up its nose and then be carried away as the animal took off like a rocket. They were thrown about like dolls, but they never let go. The thing that really shook me was the way that their cigarettes still hung in their mouths.

It grew as hot as an oven in the buildings, and the animals sprayed us with non-stop jets of muck. The brothers stopped work and laughed loudly when a cow hit me in the face with her mucky tail. In moments of stress they swore softly: 'Get off my bloody foot you old bitch.' They thought it was very funny when a bullock crashed his behind into my middle, just as I was filling up the syringe. The wind shot out of me in a hiccup. Then the beast squashed me against the wall like a fly.

We did the smallest calves last. The shaggy little beasts kicked, sprang in the air, and ran through our legs. Often the brothers had to sit on top of them to keep them down so that I could give them their shots. When the calves felt the needle they stuck out their tongues and screamed. Their worried mothers stood outside and cried in sympathy.

What a job! We finished at noon. It seemed as if I had been in with the cattle and their heat, noise and muck for a month. I had a quick clean up in a bucket of water, then I drove home.

On the way, I stopped and got out of the car for some fresh air. I took off my sweaty shirt, and sat in the sun, on the fell-side. It was a lovely day.

I smiled to myself and thought what a funny way to earn a living. My ribs ached and my legs were covered with bruises. But it was much better than being in an office. I thought of what an office job would be like. The window would be shut, with the noise of traffic outside and the smell of petrol, my desk full of papers to be worked on.

No, life wasn't too bad. . . .

9   A fine mistake

The time rushed past. I soon began to feel at home.

Most days I had a puncture. The tyres were bald on all the wheels. I was surprised I got anywhere at all. The car had a sunshine roof. I kept it open most of the time, and the windows too. I drove with my shirt sleeves rolled up, and loved the fresh, cool air on my skin. On wet days there was no point in shutting the roof. The rain leaked through everywhere, anyhow, and made pools of water on my lap.

I got very good at making zig-zags round puddles. It was a mistake to drive through them, as water shot up between the gaps in the floor boards. But it was a fine summer and soon I had a tan as good as the farmers'. And my boss was very interesting to get to know.

Siegfried was a ball of energy from dawn till dusk. It was not money that drove him on. He never thought about it. When people paid their bills the money went into the pint pot on the shelf, and he grabbed a handful when he wanted it. His pockets were full of loose change and screwed up notes.

Every morning he made a quick list of calls for me. The speed at which he did it led to mistakes, of course. Often I was sent off to the wrong farm or to do the wrong job. Afterwards, when I told him, he would think it was very funny.

Once he was caught in the same way. It happened like this. I had just taken a call from a Mr Heaton who wanted me to examine a dead sheep for him.

'I'd like to come with you, James,' Siegfried said. 'Things are quiet this morning and I want to see you in action.'

We drove into the right village and Siegfried turned left.

'Where are you going?' I asked. 'Heaton's is at the other end of the village.'

'But you said Seaton's,' he said. I said that I had not.

'Look James, I was right by you when you were talking to the man.' I opened my mouth to argue, but then I decided to let him find out for himself.

We stopped outside the farm-house. Siegfried got out of the car and began hunting in the boot of the car for a knife to cut open the sheep. He could not find it. He slammed down the lid and went towards the farm to borrow one.

The farmer's wife came to the door and Siegfried asked her for a sharp knife. She looked surprised, but sent her little girl in to get one. After some time the little girl came back with a sharp-looking knife.

Siegfried tested it on his hand.

'This is no good!' he shouted. 'Fetch me a steel to sharpen it.'

The girl ran back into the kitchen. Some minutes later another little girl, looking very scared, came back with a steel. Then she ran back indoors as fast as she could.

Siegfried made a good job of sharpening the knife. He sang at the top of his voice as he did it.

When he had finished he looked inside the door and called, 'Where is your husband?'

There was no reply, so he went into the kitchen, waving the knife over his head. I followed him. Mrs Seaton and her little girls were trying to hide in the far corner. They stared at Siegfried with big scared eyes.

Siegfried said to them, 'Well, come on, I can get started now!'

'Start what?' asked the mother with horror, holding her family close to her.

'I want to open up this dead sheep. You have got a dead sheep, haven't you?' asked Siegfried. Mrs Seaton said no, and slowly the mistake was explained.

On the way home in the car Siegfried said,

'You must be more careful, James. That sort of mistake looks bad.'

10   Siegfried blows his top

I got used to Siegfried's changes of mind. There was one morning when he came down to breakfast rubbing his tired eyes.

'Out at four this morning,' he said, 'and I don't like to have to say this, but it's all your fault.'

'My fault?' I said, surprised.

'Yes, lad. This was a cow with a blocked teat. The farmer had been mucking about with it for days. A bit of this, a bit of that, and then at four in the morning he decides to call the vet. When I pointed out that it could have waited a few hours more, he told me that Mr Herriot had told him never to wait to ring. You told him that you would go out any hour of the day or night.'

'I'm very sorry, Siegfried. Maybe it's just because I'm new. If I didn't go out I'd be scared the animal might die,' I said.

'You mustn't worry,' snapped Siegfried. 'There's nothing like a dead animal to bring them to their senses. They would call us out a bit sooner the next time.'

I thought about this and tried to act on it. A week later Siegfried said he wanted a word with me.

'James, I had a complaint from Sumner today. He

says he rang you the other night and you wouldn't go out to his cow. He's a good payer you know, and a very nice fellow. He was quite angry about it.'

'But it was only a touch of milk fever,' I said. 'The cow was eating all right, so I thought it would be quite safe to leave it till the next day.'

Siegfried put a hand on my arm. A patient look came on his face.

'James,' he said in a gentle voice, 'the most important rule in our job is – *you must visit*. Always remember that. No matter what, if it's wet or fine, night or day. If you are called out, you must go. Don't forget, the animal may take a turn for the worse, and die.'

'But I thought you said there was nothing like a dead animal to bring the farmers to their senses?' I asked.

Siegfried looked at me in great surprise. 'Never heard such rubbish. Let's have no more of it. Just remember – *you must visit*.'

Sometimes he would tell me how to put up with life when it got tough.

One day he found me sitting by the phone, which I had just crashed down. When he heard me swearing he asked me what was the matter. I told him that I had just spent half an hour talking to a client who was not very happy about his bill. I was angry because I had spent hours with the man's sick animals, and had been very pleased with myself that none of them had died. However, the client was not at all grateful for all my hard work.

Siegfried put on his patient look again. 'My dear chap, you mustn't let yourself get upset like this. You must learn to take these things in your stride. Keep calm, James. It isn't worth getting all steamed up. It will all be the same in a hundred years,' he said, and smiled.

I was writing a label on a jar in the dispensary a few days later. Suddenly, Siegfried came into the room. He kicked the door open, and rushed over to the desk where I sat. He began to bang on it with the flat of his hand. His eyes glared and his face was red.

'I've just come from that bloody swine Holt!' he shouted.

I was surprised, and said, 'I thought he was one of your favourites?'

'Not now,' Siegfried shouted. 'I've been treating one of his cows for him. She's been coming in from the field every night in great pain. After a while, I thought it must be a bug, so I gave her a shot of something. It seemed to work. When I saw her today she was standing there chewing the cud, right as rain. I was just patting myself on the back, and do you know what Holt said? He said he knew she would be better today because last night he gave her half a pound of Epsom salts in her mash. That was what had cured her.'

Siegfried took some empty boxes and bottles from his pocket and threw them into the waste-paper basket. He began to shout again.

'Do you know, for the last two weeks I have thought of nothing but that cow. Now I've found out what the trouble is, given it the right medicine and the cow is better. And what happens? The owner thinks he's done all the work with half a pound of Epsom salts. What I did was a waste of time.'

He hit the desk very hard and went on, 'But I scared him, James, I really scared him. When he made that crack about the salts I yelled at him and made a grab at him. He shot into the house and stayed there. I didn't see him again.'

I thought of telling Siegfried to relax. I felt like saying that it would all be the same in a hundred years. But he still had an empty bottle in his hand, so I didn't.

11   A bit of a joke

I was now happy and settled in my life at Darrowby.
At first I wondered where Tristan fitted into the set-
up. Was he having a holiday, helping us with the
work, or what? But it was soon clear he was the odd-
job man. He made up the medicines and took them
out to the farmers. He washed the cars, took the phone
calls and even went on a case in an emergency.

At least, that is what Siegfried had in mind for him.
What I could not understand was why he was not back
at college. Surely the holidays were over by now?

Tristan did not see his job in the same way as
Siegfried. Tristan's main idea was to do as little as
possible. He spent much of his time sleeping in a chair.
When Siegfried came into the room, Tristan would
start to shake a medicine bottle wildly. He hoped
Siegfried would think that he had been busy mixing
medicine for ages.

Most evenings he spent sitting on a high stool at the
pub talking to the barmaid. At other times he would
be out with one of the nurses from the local hospital.
All in all, he seemed to be having a good time.

Saturday night, half past ten. The phone rang. I
swore to myself as I lifted the phone up.

'Hello, Herriot speaking,' I said.

'I want Mr Farnon,' said a cross voice.

'I'm sorry, Mr Farnon is out,' I said. 'Can I help you?'

'Well, I hope so, but I'd far rather have your boss. This is Sims of Beal Close.'

(Oh, no, please no, I thought, not Beal Close. Miles up in the hills at the end of a rough lane with about eight farm gates to get out and open.)

'Yes, Mr Sims, and what is your trouble?' I said aloud.

'I'll say there's some trouble. I have a great big show horse here. He's cut his hind leg badly. Just above the hock. He needs stitches straight away.'

'How big is the wound, Mr Sims?' I asked.

'Big? It's a great big thing about a foot long, and bleeding like hell. I can't get near him at all. Goes right up the wall when he sees anybody.'

I didn't feel too happy as I said, 'Well, I'll be along right away.'

'Oh, I nearly forgot,' he said, 'my road got washed away by the floods yesterday. You'll have to walk the last mile and a half. So get a move on, and don't keep me waiting all night.'

This was a bit much, so I said, 'Look here, Mr Sims, I don't like your tone. I will get there as soon as I can.'

'You don't like my tone, eh? Well, I don't like stupid young fools working on my good stock. So I don't want any cheek from you. You don't know anything about the job anyway.'

That did it. 'Now listen to me, Sims. If it wasn't for your horse, I wouldn't come out at all,' I said. 'Who do you think you are? If you speak to me like that again . . .'

The voice at the end of the phone changed. 'Now, now, Jim, don't take on so. You'll have to watch that temper of yours.'

'Who the devil . . .?' I said, and then I knew.

'Tristan! Where the hell are you speaking from?'

'The pub. I've got five pints inside me and I felt full of fun. Thought I'd give you a ring.'

To play a joke like that was Tristan's idea of fun. I said: 'By God, I'll kill you one of these days if you don't stop pretending to be other people. It's putting years on me. Now and again isn't so bad, but this is the third time this week,' I said.

'But it was the best so far, Jim,' said Tristan. 'It nearly killed me. I wish you could have heard yourself.' He laughed and laughed.

I tried to get my own back, but it never worked. I would creep into some phone box and say in a strange voice, 'Is that young Mr Farnon? I want you to come out right away. I've got a bad case of . . .'

But Tristan would say quickly,

'Jim, is there something wrong with your voice? Good. What were you saying, old lad?'

12 Doing a favour

'You want Mr Herriot? OK. I'll get him for you,'
said Siegfried into the telephone. 'Come on, James.
Here's another one who likes you better than me,' he
said as he handed the phone to me. He was smiling.
He looked pleased.

As I took the phone I thought some bosses might not
have been so happy to be passed over for their assistant.
And I thought, too, of how some of the farmers
had changed in the last few weeks. They didn't look
past me now hoping that Siegfried had come with me.
They had got used to me. This really meant something
to me. I was getting very fond of the people of the
Dales.

This Sunday morning it was the Bellerbys calling.
They lived at the top of a little valley high up in the
Dale. My car bumped and rattled over the last rough
mile. Rocks stuck up out of the track every few yards.

The cow shed was dark. The walls were thick and
the windows were small. I went in. At first I could not
see, but my eyes soon got used to the dark. There stood
a cow with a label tied to its tail. People often left
messages for the vet in this way. I looked at the label.
It said, 'Milk fever.'

I pushed the cow over and began to look at its teats.

I began to draw out the sticky, dark milk. I looked up and saw Ruth Bellerby at the door. She was a fine-looking woman in her late thirties. She was no fool.

'Oh, I'm so glad it's you, Mr Herriot,' she said. 'I hoped you'd come so that I could ask you a favour.'

'I'll be glad to help you if I can, Miss Bellerby. What would you like me to do?' I asked.

'Would you give us a lift in your car into Darrowby?' she asked. 'There's a concert at the church that we'd all like to go to. We could go in the pony and trap, but it's so slow. If you gave us a ride in I'm sure someone would give us a lift back,' she said. I said that I'd be glad to and that I was going to the concert myself.

It was good to be able to help people like this. They were always so kind. They were never in a hurry. They got up when it was light and went to bed when they were tired. They ate when they were hungry and did not look at the clock very often.

Ruth led the way over to the house. 'There's just mother and dad and me going,' she said. 'Bob doesn't want to go, I'm afraid.'

I was surprised when I went in. The family were just sitting down to Sunday dinner. They were still in their working clothes. I looked at my watch: a quarter to twelve. The concert started at two o'clock. Oh well, I probably had plenty of time.

'Come on, young man,' said little Mr Bellerby. 'Sit down and have a bit of dinner.'

I thanked him, but said that my own dinner would be ready for me when I got back home. Mrs Hall would not like it if I let it go to waste. They understood this. Then they all sat down round the kitchen table.

Mrs Bellerby gave each of them a big Yorkshire

pudding. She poured a pool of gravy over each pudding from a big jug. I had had a hard morning, and the good smell of the food made me feel very hungry. Still, I told myself, they would hurry because I was sitting waiting for them.

It was quiet as they slowly ate their pudding. Then Bob, a big thickset man of about twenty, pushed out his empty plate. He did not say anything, but his mother put another pudding on the plate, and poured on more gravy. The rest of the family sat and smiled at him as he ate his second pudding.

Next a huge roast came out of the oven. Mr Bellerby cut at it till they all had a heap of thick slices on their plates. Then mountains of mashed potato were served from a pan as big as a washing up bowl. Chopped turnip was piled on the top and then the family began to eat again.

There was no sign of haste. They ate slowly and quietly, without any small talk. Bob had an extra helping of potatoes. The family were happy but I wasn't. I was very hungry, and the time was ticking away.

There was a wait. Then Mrs Bellerby went over to the oven, opened the door and pulled out a great flat tin of apple pie. She then cut about a square foot for each of them. Over this she poured nearly a pint of custard. The family set to as though they were just starting the meal. Bob pushed his plate forward when it was empty, and had another huge helping.

It was going to be a close thing, I thought, but this must now be the end. They would see that time was getting short, and go and change. But to my horror, Mrs Bellerby moved to the fire and put the kettle on.

Bob and his father sat back in their chairs. Bob took out a cigarette and lay back smoking happily as his mother put a cup of tea in front of him. Mr Bellerby smoked his pipe.

They sat around the table sipping their hot tea slowly. I felt very tense. My head ached, my heart beat quickly. I had all the usual signs of worry.

After a second cup of tea they began to move. Mr Bellerby rose from his chair and said, 'Well, young man, we'll just have a bit of a wash and get changed. Bob will stay and talk to you. He's not coming with us.'

There was a lot of splashing in the big stone sink at the far end of the kitchen. Then they went upstairs. It did not take them long to change. They looked very smart in their best clothes.

'All ready, then?' I said. 'Right, off we go. After you, ladies.'

But Ruth did not move. As she put on her gloves she said to her brother, 'Bob, it makes my blood boil to look at you. As soon as we are out of that door you'll be asleep. Snoring like a pig all afternoon. Mother! I've made up my mind. I'm not going to leave him here. He's got to come with us!'

I felt the sweat on my brow. I wanted my lunch, and we were already late. Before I could get a word in Ruth said, 'Get up out of there, Bob! Get ready to come with us!'

She was too much for Bob. He did not seem to have much of a mind of his own. He looked sulky, but went over to the sink. The family sat down and watched him wash. For my own part, I was only just stopping myself from going mad. I wanted to jump up and down and scream at the top of my voice. I shut my eyes to try and control my nerves. I must have kept them closed for a long time, because when I opened them again Bob was ready.

I do not remember much about the ride to Darrowby. I have only a faint idea of the car roaring down the stony track at forty miles an hour. The family, packed in tightly, seemed to enjoy the ride.

I shot in the house at ten to two and out again at two. Mrs Hall, the housekeeper, was angry but silent as I bolted her good food.

I was late for the concert. The music had started as I crept into the church. I could see by people's faces that they were shocked at my lateness. Out of the corner of my eye I could see the Bellerby family. They looked more shocked than anyone else.

13 An old dog

In Darrowby there were a lot of little streets behind the shops in the market square. They were called yards. It always surprised me to go down a passage between two shops, and find a row of little houses.

One morning I made my way into one of these yards. I looked again at the slip of paper on which I had written my visits. 'Dean, 3 Thompson's Yard. Old dog ill.' Number three was at the end of the yard. It looked in a bad state, almost falling down.

A small, white-haired old man opened the door. His face was pinched and lined, but his eyes were bright. I saw that his clothes were old and shabby.

'I've come to see your dog,' I said. The old man smiled.

'I'm glad you've come, sir. I'm a bit worried about the old chap. Come inside please.' He led me into the tiny living-room.

'I'm alone now, sir. Lost my wife over a year ago. She used to think the world of the old dog,' he said. From the state of the room I could see now poor he was. The lino was worn out. There was no fire in the grate. The wallpaper was hanging off the walls. On the table was the old man's dinner, a scrap of bacon, a few chips and a cup of tea. This was life on the old age pension.

The dog was on a rug in the corner. I could see from the white hair round his mouth that he was old. He lay quiet and looked at me in a friendly way.

'How old is he, Mr Dean?' I asked.

'Getting on for fourteen, sir, but he's been like a pup until these last few weeks. Wonderful dog for his age, is old Bob. Never tried to bite anyone in his life. He's my only friend now. I hope you'll soon be able to put him right,' the old man said.

I asked, 'Is he off his food, Mr Dean?'

He replied, 'Yes, right off. He always sat by me with his head on my knee at meal times, waiting for a scrap. But he does not do that now.'

I looked at the dog. I could tell he was in pain. Whenever his master spoke he wagged his tail. For a moment he looked interested in what was going on, but soon he lost interest, and the blank look came back in his old eyes.

I passed my hand over the dog's stomach. It was very swollen. 'Come on, old chap,' I said. 'Let's see if we can roll you over.' I gently rolled him over on to his other side. The trouble was now only too easy to find.

I felt his side gently. I could feel a huge hard lump. It was a cancer, and it was too late to do anything about it. I stroked the old dog's head as I tried to think what to say. This was not going to be easy.

'Is he going to be ill for long?' the old man asked. Again the old dog wagged his tail at the sound of the loved voice.

'I'm sorry, Mr Dean, but I'm afraid this is very bad.

You see this lump? It is a growth inside the dog,' I said.

'You mean cancer?' the little man said very softly.

'I'm afraid so. I wish there was something I could do, but there isn't,' I said.

The old man looked at me. His lip trembled. He said,

'Then he's going to die?' I felt a lump in my throat.

'We really can't just leave him to die, can we?' I said. 'He's in pain now, but it will soon be an awful lot worse. Don't you think it would be kindest to put him to sleep?'

The old man said, 'Just a minute.' He slowly got down by the dog. He did not speak, but ran his hand again and again over the grey ears and head. The old dog's tail went thump, thump on the floor at the feel of his master's hand.

After a long time the old man got to his feet. Without looking at me he said, 'All right. Will you do it now?'

I got ready to give the dog an injection.

'He won't feel a thing. It is really an easy way out for the old chap,' I told Mr Dean.

The dog did not move when the needle went in. By the time the syringe was empty the dog had stopped breathing.

'Is that it?' the old man asked.

'Yes, that's it. He's out of his pain now,' I said.

The old man turned to me. His eyes were bright with tears. He said, 'That's right. We couldn't let him suffer. Thank you for what you did. And now how much do I owe you?'

Quickly I told him that I did not want any money. He looked surprised, but I told him I was just going past his door on the way to another job. I said good-bye and went out of the house, through the passage and into the street.

As I walked to my car, I heard a shout behind me. The old man was coming towards me in his slippers. He smiled at me and held something out to me. It was small and brown.

'You've been very kind, sir. I've got something for you.' It was old and bent, a treat saved from last Christmas, perhaps.

'Go on. It's for you,' said the old man. 'Have a cigar.'

14   Tricki Woo

During my first winter in Darrowby I found my work hard. When the snow came I began to learn how nasty life could be for a vet in the country.

I drove for hours with frozen feet. I climbed to the high barns in biting winds. I always had to strip off to work in freezing buildings. Then I had to wash my hands and chest in a bucket of cold water.

My hands were badly chapped. When there was a rush of work on, they were never really dry. My skin was cracked and red right up to the elbow.

This was when I was glad to have some work with pets. It was good to walk into a warm room instead of a cold cow-shed, to look after a small animal instead of fighting with a large horse or bull. And the nicest person to visit was Mrs Pumfrey.

Mrs Pumfrey was a widow. Her husband had left her a lot of money and a lovely house on the edge of Darrowby. Here she lived with her servants, and Tricki Woo. Tricki Woo was her Peke, and the apple of her eye.

I was always careful to visit her half an hour before lunch. I knew she would give me a glass or two of her splendid sherry at that time. She would also ask me to sit in a deep armchair close to a warm fire.

As I stood at her grand front door one bitter cold morning I thought of all this. The maid who came to the door smiled at me. She knew I was a friend of Tricki Woo. She led me into the room where Mrs Pumfrey sat in her high-backed armchair by the fire. When she saw me she put down her book with a cry of delight.

'Tricki! Tricki!' she called. 'Here is your Uncle Herriot!'

I had been made an uncle early on. I saw that it would be a good thing for me, so I had not minded. Tricki, as usual, jumped up from his cushion. He got on to the back of a sofa and put his paws on my shoulders. He then licked my face all over, and sat down again, tired out. He was tired out so soon because he was given about twice as much food as he needed for a dog of his size. And it was the wrong kind of food.

'Oh, Mr Herriot, I'm so glad you've come. Tricki has got flop-bott again,' Mrs Pumfrey said.

That was what Mrs Pumfrey called her dog's usual trouble. Quite often the glands on Tricki Woo's behind got blocked. When these glands do not empty, the dog feels very uncomfortable. Tricki would show this by sitting down suddenly in the middle of his walk. Then Mrs Pumfrey would rush to the phone and say to me, 'Mr Herriot, please come quickly! Tricki Woo has got flop-bott again!'

I put the little dog on a table and pressed his glands with some cotton wool. This made them empty. It always surprised me that the Peke was so pleased to see me. Tricki did not seem to mind that every time he saw me I grabbed hold of him and squeezed his bottom. In fact he was a very good tempered little animal. He was very bright, and I really did like him.

As I lifted him down from the table I saw how much weight he had put on. I said, 'You know, Mrs Pumfrey, you are giving him too much to eat again. Didn't I tell you to cut out all the cake?'

'Oh yes, Mr Herriot,' said Mrs Pumfrey. 'But what can I do? He's so tired of chicken.' It was hopeless.

The maid led me to a beautiful bathroom, where I washed my hands. Then I went back to the room where Mrs Pumfrey filled my sherry glass. I sat down in the armchair to listen to her.

She did all the talking but I did not mind listening to her. Mrs Pumfrey was a nice person. She was very kind and would help anyone in trouble. She was clever and funny, but her one blind spot was Tricki Woo. It was not possible to believe the stories she told about her darling, but it was funny to listen to them.

I sat back and sipped my sherry. Tricki slept on my lap. Mrs Pumfrey talked on. This, I thought, was the good life.

'I had such a fright last week,' she said. 'I was sure I would have to call you out. Poor old Tricki – he went "crackerdog"!'

'That's a new one on me,' I thought.

Mrs Pumfrey went on, 'It was awful. I was really scared. The gardener was throwing rings for Tricki. You know he does this for half an hour every day. Well, Tricki was playing his game, when suddenly he went "crackerdog". He forgot all about his rings. He began to run round in circles. He barked and barked in such a strange way. Then he lay on his side like a dead thing. I really thought he was dead, he lay so still. It was horrid. I was just going to rush for the phone when Tricki got up and walked away. He seemed quite normal again.'

I thought it must have been a fit. Too much food and too much rushing around for a fat dog. I put down my glass and looked sternly at Mrs Pumfrey.

'Now look, this is just what I'm talking about,' I said to her. 'If you go on giving Tricki the wrong things to eat you are going to make him ill. You must get him on to a good diet. One or two small meals a day of meat and brown bread or a biscuit. And nothing in between.'

Mrs Pumfrey looked very sad and said, 'Oh, please don't speak to me like that. I do try to give him the right things, but it is hard. When he begs for something nice I can't say no.'

But I wouldn't give up. 'All right, Mrs Pumfrey, it's up to you,' I said. 'I warn you if you go on doing as you are doing, Tricki will go "crackerdog" more and more often.' When it was time to go I did not want to leave the cosy room. I stopped to wave at Mrs Pumfrey and Tricki, as they waved to me from the window.

As I drove home I thought of how nice it was to be Tricki's uncle. When he went to the seaside he sent me boxes of smoked kippers. When the tomatoes were ripe he sent me a pound or two every week. Tins of tobacco came often, sometimes with a photo of Tricki.

But it was when the Christmas hamper had come from a big London store that I knew I was on to a good thing. I decided that I ought to help things along a bit. Up until then I had rung up and thanked Mrs Pumfrey for the gifts. She had been rather cool and had pointed out that the gifts came from Tricki. So when the hamper came I set myself to write a letter to Tricki.

I thanked my doggy nephew for the Christmas gift. I sent him his uncle's love. I addressed the letter to Master Tricki Pumfrey and posted it.

When I next saw Mrs Pumfrey she told me how much Tricki had loved my letter. But he had been hurt because I had put 'Master' and not 'Mister' on the envelope. He hoped I would not do the same thing again! I thought of these things as I went back to the real, cold world.

I bumped into Siegfried as I went into the house.

'Ah, who have we here?' he said. 'Why, I think it's dear Uncle Herriot. And what have you been doing, Uncle? Slaving away for poor Tricki I expect. Poor fellow, you must be worn out. Do you really think it's worth it, working your fingers to the bone for another Christmas hamper?'

15 Miss Harbottle

In those days we used to mix up our own medicines. Our drugs did not come to us in boxes from the makers. Before we could get out on the road we had to fill our cars with all sort of bottles.

One morning Tristan and I were busy mixing up medicines when Siegfried came in. He smiled to see us both working so hard. I smiled too. It was not easy for me being around when there was trouble between the brothers. But I could see that this was going to be one of the happy mornings. Things had been much better since Christmas. Tristan had gone back to college and re-sat and passed his exams, without any fuss.

Today Siegfried looked very pleased with himself.

'I've got some good news,' he said. 'We're going to have a secretary.'

As we stared at him he went on, 'Yes. I picked her myself and I think she's perfect.'

I asked him what she was like.

'It's hard to say,' he replied, 'but just think – what do we want here? We don't want anyone who is too young and pretty sitting behind that desk.'

Tristan did not look at all sure about this, which seemed to make Siegfried angry. His face went red and he shouted, 'How could we have a pretty girl in here with somebody like you in the house? You'd never leave her alone.'

I closed my eyes. The peace had not lasted long.

'Tell us about her then, Siegfried,' I said.

He calmed down and said, 'Well, she's about fifty. She has just retired from a big firm in Bradford. I've had a very good letter from the firm about her. It's just a stroke of luck, for us that she's come to live in Darrowby. Anyway, you'll meet her in a few minutes. She's coming at ten o'clock this morning.'

The church bell was ringing when the door bell rang. Siegfried rushed to open it. He led her in to meet us, saying, 'Gentlemen, meet Miss Harbottle.'

She was a big, stout woman with a round healthy face and gold glasses. I thought, we won't have to worry about Tristan rushing after her. It was not that she was ugly, but she had the air of someone used to giving orders. She would send any man running for his life.

I shook hands. I wasn't surprised at her strong grip. Tristan did not expect such strength, and a look of alarm came over his face as she grabbed his hand. She let go only when his knees started to bend.

Miss Harbottle began a tour of the office with Siegfried. She stopped at the desk. On it were heaps of in-coming and out-going bills, forms from the Ministry of Agriculture, letters from drug firms and boxes of pills and tubes of cream. She picked up a shabby old book from the mess. 'What's this?' she asked.

Siegfried moved forward to explain. 'Oh, that's our ledger. We enter the visits in it from our day book. That's here too somewhere.' He hunted for it in the mess. 'Ah, here it is. This is where we write the calls when they come in.'

She looked at the two books for a few moments. She looked shocked. Then she said with a grim smile, 'You gentlemen will have to learn to write better if I'm going to look after your books.' Siegfried hung his head in shame. We all knew that his was the worst hand-writing of the three of us.

'I expect you keep your paper and envelopes in here,' said Miss Harbottle. She pulled open a drawer in the desk. It seemed to be full of old seed packets. Many of them had burst open. The next drawer was full of dirty, very smelly, rope. She shut the drawer quickly. She opened the third drawer. It was full of empty beer bottles.

'And where is your cash box, Mr Farnon?' she asked. Siegfried pointed to the pint pot on the shelf.

He said, 'We just stuff the money in there. It does the job all right.' Miss Harbottle looked at the pot in horror.

'And you mean to say you go out and leave that money there all day?' she asked.

'Never seems to come to any harm,' Siegfried said.

Miss Harbottle's red face had lost some of its colour. 'Really, Mr Farnon, this is too bad. I don't know how you have gone on so long like this. Still, I'm sure I shall soon be able to put things to rights.'

'Fine, Miss Harbottle, fine,' said Siegfried. 'Well, see you on Monday morning, then?'

She said, 'Nine o'clock sharp, Mr Farnon,' and left.

'Don't you think she's a bit tough, Siegfried?' I said.

'Tough?' Siegfried gave a laugh. 'Not a bit of it. You leave her to me. I can handle her.'

16 Siegfried has an idea

Tristan and I sat eating our breakfast. The window was covered in frost. In the street the feet of the people who passed by crunched in the soft snow. I looked up from my boiled egg as a car drew up outside. I heard stamping in the porch. The front door banged shut, and Siegfried burst into the room. Without a word he made for the fire. He had on a big overcoat and warm scarf, but his face was blue with cold.

He had been high up in the hills. A farmer had called him out in the middle of the night. As he pulled off his gloves and shook his hands in front of the fire, he kept looking at his brother. Tristan's chair was very near the fire. He was enjoying his breakfast. He was reading the *Daily Mirror*. He looked very pleased with life.

Siegfried sat down in a chair and said, 'I'll just have a cup of coffee, please, James. The farmer was very kind. He asked me to sit down and have breakfast with him. He gave me a lovely slice of home fed bacon. I can taste it now. You know, there's no reason why we should have to buy bacon and eggs. We've got a good hen house at the bottom of the garden, and there's a pig sty, too. We could feed a pig with the scraps from the house.'

Tristan lit a cigarette and went on reading his *Daily Mirror*.

Siegfried said to him, 'It would be a useful thing for you to do. You're not doing much, sitting on your behind all day.' Tristan put down his paper and pointed out that he already fed Siegfried's horse every day. (He didn't like doing this, as the horse was very fond of kicking him, if he got the chance.)

'I know you do,' said Siegfried, 'it doesn't take all day, does it? It won't hurt you to take on the hens and the pigs.'

'Pigs?' Tristan looked surprised. 'I thought you said pig?'

'Yes, pigs,' said Siegfried. 'I've just been thinking. If I buy a litter of piglets we can sell them, but keep one for us. Won't cost us a penny that way.' Tristan said it was true, they would not cost anything, as long as he did all the work.

Siegfried looked angry. 'Work? You don't know the meaning of the word,' he yelled. 'Look at you, puffing your head off. You smoke too many of those damn cigarettes!'

'So do you,' Tristan said.

'Never mind me, I'm talking about you!' Siegfried shouted. I got up from the table with a sigh. The day had begun.

17   Trouble for Tristan

When Siegfried got an idea he didn't muck about. Two days later ten little pigs were in the sty. Ten little hens pecked about behind the wire of the hen house. Siegfried was very pleased with the hens.

He said to me, 'Look at them, James. They are just about to start laying. Only a few eggs, at first, but they'll soon get going. Nothing like a nice fresh egg warm from the nest.'

Right from the first it was plain that Tristan was not keen on the hens. He did not seem to feed them as often as he should have done. There were no eggs as the weeks passed. Siegfried got more and more angry. It was sad to see him looking in the empty nesting boxes every morning.

One afternoon I was in the garden when Tristan called me. He pointed up to the branches of the trees. On the branches I saw a group of strange big birds. Tristan laughed at my surprised face and said:

'They're our hens!'

'How the devil did they get up there?' I asked.

'They've left home,' he replied. 'Hopped it.' I pointed out that I could only see five of them, so we looked over the garden wall. The other five hens were pecking about happily among some cabbages.

It took a long time to get them back into the hen house. We found we had to get them back in the hen house many times a day from that day onwards. The hens seemed to have grown tired of living with us. They began to wander further and further away, looking for food.

At first the people who lived nearby laughed. They phoned to say their children were rounding up our hens, and could we come and get them. Soon they began to get fed up. They told Siegfried that his hens were giving them a lot of trouble.

Siegfried knew that the hens must go. It was a bitter blow to him. He blamed Tristan, of course, and said to him, 'I must have been mad to think that any hens in your care would ever lay eggs. Not one egg in three weeks. The blasted hens fly about the town like pigeons. Nobody who lives near will speak to us. You've done a good job, haven't you?'

Siegfried gave the hens to an old lady who lived nearby.

One day, about a fortnight later, I was sitting at the dining table with Tristan. I felt sure that all was forgotten about the hens. Suddenly Siegfried came into the room, looking angry.

'You remember those hens?' he said. 'Well, I've just been talking to the old lady I gave them to. She's very pleased with them. She gives them a hot mash every day, night and morning. They are laying ten eggs a day. Do you hear that, Tristan? Ten eggs a day!'

Quickly I finished my tea and went out. I went out

of the back door, across the garden to my car. On the way I passed the empty hen house. It was a long way to the dining-room, but I could still hear Siegfried shouting at Tristan.

18   Ten little pigs

Right from the start Tristan liked the pigs better than the hens. He spent a lot of time feeding the pigs, or mucking them out, or just looking at them. Each time he poured the swill into the long trough he watched them eat with great interest. First of all the pigs made a rush for the trough. Then each one wanted to know what the others had found to eat. They would begin to change places, climbing over each other and falling in the swill. It was funny to watch.

As the weeks passed the piglets grew with great speed. They soon became very solid, big pigs. They lost all their charm. Meal times stopped being fun for Tristan. They became a battle. The pigs would squeal when they heard the rattle of their food bucket. Tristan would then bravely open the door of the sty, and push himself among the grunting pigs. They forced their greedy noses into the bucket, trod on Tristan's feet, and pushed their heavy bodies against his legs.

I couldn't help smiling when I remembered the game it used to be. There was no laughter now. In the end Tristan used to take a heavy stick into the sty with him. Once inside his only hope of staying on his feet was to clear a little space for himself by beating the pigs back.

One market day when the pigs were almost the right weight for killing for bacon I came in to find Tristan in an armchair. There was something strange about him. He was not asleep, he was not smoking and he was not reading the *Daily Mirror*. His eyes were half-shut and he was sweating.

He said, 'Jim, I've just had the worst afternoon of my life.' I was worried about him, and asked what had happened.

He went on, 'The pigs got out today. It was when I was feeding Siegfried's horse. I gave her some hay, and thought I might as well feed the pigs at the same time. You know what they've been like lately? Well, today they went mad. As soon as I opened the door they charged out. Sent me up in the air, bucket and all. Then they ran over the top of me. I'll tell you, Jim, when I was lying there, covered in swill, pigs running all over me, I thought it was all over. But they didn't attack me. They ran out of the door at full gallop.'

'The yard door was open?' I asked.

'Too true it was,' he said. 'Trust me to leave it open today. Anyway, they slowed down when they got into the lane. They trotted round into the street, with me chasing them. They got into a group there. Didn't seem to know which way to go next. I was sure I was going to be able to head them off. Just then, though, one of them saw itself in a shop window.

'That did it, Jim. The stupid animal went mad and shot off into the market place at about fifty miles an hour with the rest after it.'

I gasped. Ten large pigs loose among the stalls and market day crowds was an awful thought.

'Oh, God, you should have seen it.' Tristan went on

with his story. 'Women and kids screaming. The stall holders, police and everybody else cursing me. There was a traffic jam, too. Miles of cars tooting like hell while the policeman on point duty gave me a good telling off.'

I asked him if he had got them back.

'I've got nine of them back. With the help of almost all of the men in Darrowby. The tenth was last seen heading north at a fast gallop. God knows where it is now. Oh, I didn't tell you, one of them got into the post office. Spent quite some time there.'

Tristan put his hands over his face, and went on, 'I'm in for it this time, Jim. The police will be on to me after this lot. There's no doubt about it.'

I tried to cheer him up by saying that there really did not sound as if much damage was done.

Tristan replied with a groan, 'But there's something else. When I shut the door after getting the pigs back in the sty I saw that the horse was gone. I'd gone straight out after the pigs and forgot to shut her box. I don't know where she is. This is the end, Jim. Siegfried won't forgive me this time.' He lit a cigarette with a shaking hand.

Suddenly the door flew open and Siegfried rushed in. 'What the hell's going on?' he shouted. 'I've just been speaking to the vicar. He says my horse is in his garden, eating his flowers. He's hopping mad, and I don't blame him. Go on, you lazy hog, don't sit there. Go over and get my horse back this minute!'

Tristan did not move. All he said was 'no' in a faint voice. Siegfried could not believe his ears. 'Get out and get that horse!' he yelled.

'No,' said Tristan again. I felt a chill of horror.

Siegfried went very red in the face, but it was Tristan who spoke. 'If you want your horse go and get her yourself.' His voice was quiet. He looked as if he did not care what happened.

Even Siegfried could see that Tristan had had enough. Siegfried glared at his brother, then turned and walked out. He got the horse himself.

Nothing more was said about the pigs. Very soon they were taken to the bacon factory. Siegfried did not buy any more pigs.

19   Miss Harbottle gets to work

When I came in Miss Harbottle was sitting looking into the empty cash box. She looked sad. It was a new, shiny, black box with the words 'Petty Cash' on top. Inside was a red book with neat lines drawn in it. But there was no money.

'He's been at it again,' Miss Harbottle said to me. We heard somebody in the passage. Miss Harbottle called out,

'Mr Farnon!' Then she said to me, 'It's really too silly the way the man tries to skip past the door.'

Siegfried came in. He smiled happily, but I could see that he was uneasy.

'Good morning, Miss Harbottle,' he said. 'Can I do anything for you?'

'You can indeed, Mr Farnon. You can tell me why once again you have emptied my petty cash box,' she said.

'Oh, I'm so sorry,' he replied. 'I had to rush out last night and I found myself a bit short of money.'

She looked at him very hard and then said, 'Mr Farnon, in the two months I have been here we must have talked about this a dozen times. What is the good of me trying to keep the books right, when you keep stealing and spending the money?'

Siegfried said, 'Well, I must have got into the habit in the old pint pot days. It wasn't a bad idea, really.'

Miss Harbottle looked angry again. 'You can not run a business that way. I've told you this so many times before. I feel almost at my wit's end,' she said.

'Never mind, Miss Harbottle. Get some more out of the bank. Put it in your box. That'll put it right,' Siegfried said, and turned to go, but Miss Harbottle had not finished.

'There are one or two other matters. Will you please try to write your visits in the book every day, and to price them as you do so. You have not written anything in for a week. How can I get the bills out on the first of the month?'

'Yes, yes, I'm sorry, but I have a string of calls waiting. I really must go.' He turned to go, and got half way across the room, when she stopped him again.

'And one more thing, Mr Farnon,' she said. 'I still can't read your writing. Please take a little more care and don't scribble.'

'Very well, Miss Harbottle,' said Siegfried, as he got through the door and into the passage. For a moment he seemed safe, but she called him back again.

Once more he stood at her desk. She wagged her finger at him and said, 'While I've got you here, there's something else I'd like to say. You see all these bits of paper, sticking out of the pages? They are all questions I have for you. There must be dozens of them. I can't get on until you answer them for me. When I ask you to do it, you never have the time. Can we go over them now?'

Siegfried backed away quickly. As he went through

the door he said to her, 'No, no, not just now. I have some urgent calls waiting. I'm very sorry. First chance I get, I'll come in and see you.'

He turned and fled.

20   An invitation

One morning I was going through the post when I came across a letter for me that did not look like the rest. Most of my letters were bills or adverts from drug firms, so I wondered who was writing to me on expensive paper. I ripped it open and pulled out an invitation card. I felt my face go red as I read it. I quickly popped it into my pocket.

But Siegfried had seen me. He laughed and began to tease me about my secret letter.

'Go on then, have a good laugh,' I said, handing him the card. 'You would find out anyway.'

Siegfried read the card aloud.

TRICKI REQUESTS THE PLEASURE OF UNCLE HERRIOT'S COMPANY.
FRIDAY FEBRUARY 5TH.   DRINKS AND DANCING.

He looked up and spoke. 'Now isn't that nice. He must be the kindest dog in England. Sending you kippers and hampers isn't enough. He has to invite you to his home for a party.'

I grabbed the card back and said, 'All right, I know. But what am I supposed to do?'

'Do? Sit down right away and write a letter saying thanks very much, you'll be there. Mrs Pumfrey's parties are famous. Masses of expensive food, rivers of champagne. Don't miss it whatever you do,' Siegfried replied.

'Will there be lots of people there?' I asked.

'Of course,' said Siegfried. 'The cream of the county will be there, dressed up to kill. But you'll be the most important person there, you know. Why? Because Mrs Pumfrey invited the others, but Tricki invited you.'

I gave a groan and said, 'I'll be on my own, and I haven't got a proper evening suit. I don't fancy it.'

Siegfried stood up and said, 'My dear chap, don't mess about. Sit down and write your letter. No problem about a suit, you can hire one for the night. You won't be on your own for long – the girls will be fighting to dance with you. And remember, don't write to Mrs Pumfrey. Write to Tricki himself or they'll *both* be hurt, and you'll be sunk.'

The day arrived. Off I went to the party in my hired suit. A maid let me into the hall. Mrs Pumfrey stood at the door of the ballroom greeting people as they arrived.

She gave me a big smile and said,

'Oh, Mr Herriot, how nice of you to come. Tricki was so pleased to get your letter. We must go in and see him now.' She led me across the hall.

'Between ourselves,' she said, 'he finds parties a bore. But he would be very cross if I didn't take you in for a moment.'

She led me into the morning-room. Tricki sat in an armchair by the fire. When he saw me he jumped on to the back of the chair. He barked, and licked my face to show how pleased he was to see me.

Then I saw two big food bowls on the carpet. In one

was about a pound of chopped chicken, and in the other a mass of cut-up cake.

'Mrs Pumfrey!' I said sternly, pointing at the bowls. The poor woman put her hand to her mouth and said, 'Oh, do forgive me. It's just a treat because he's alone tonight. And the weather is so cold too.'

'I'll forgive you if you take away half the chicken and all of the cake,' I said sternly. She did as I asked. Then we left Tricki alone in the warm room.

It had been a busy day and I was sleepy from the hours in the biting cold. Tricki's warm fire looked more inviting than the ballroom. I would have liked to stay with Tricki on my knee for an hour or two.

But Mrs Pumfrey said, 'Now you must come and meet some of my friends.' We went into the glittering ballroom. We went from group to group as Mrs Pumfrey told her friends about me. I went red as I heard her say 'This is Tricki's dear uncle.'

Waiters in white coats carried trays of food and drinks to all the people. Mrs Pumfrey stopped one of the waiters and told him to give me some champagne. He gave me a big glass.

Then she said, 'This is Mr Herriot. I want you to take a good look at him. I want you to look after him. See that his glass is full and that he has plenty to eat.'

'Certainly, Madam,' said the waiter. He bowed and moved away.

I drank the ice-cold champagne. When I looked up there was the waiter holding out a tray of smoked salmon.

It was like that all evening. The waiter seemed always to be ready to fill up my glass or push food at me. I found it all splendid. It was the first time I had drunk champagne by the pint, and I really enjoyed it. I danced with everyone in sight – rich young ladies, noble old ladies and twice with Mrs Pumfrey.

Or I just talked. How clever I am, I thought, as I talked. I wasn't at all shy any more. Once I saw myself in a mirror – tall and good-looking, I thought, in my hired suit.

The evening flew past as I ate, drank, talked and danced. When it was time to go, and I had my coat on, Mrs Pumfrey came up to me.

'And now you must come and say good night to Tricki. He'll never forgive you if you don't,' she said. We went into his room. The little dog was in his armchair. He yawned and wagged his tail.

Mrs Pumfrey said, 'While you are here, would you be so kind as to look at his claws? I worry in case they're growing too long.'

I lifted up the paws and looked at the claws one by one. Tricki licked my hands. I told her not to worry, the claws were quite all right.

Mrs Pumfrey thanked me, and then I was led away to wash my hands. There in the lovely bathroom were my own towel and expensive soap laid out for me. The water from the shiny tap was piping hot. It was the last touch of luxury to a delightful evening.

I went home. I got into bed, and put out the light. I had just fallen asleep when the phone rang.

'This is Atkinson of Beck Cottage,' a voice said. 'I have a sow here that can't get pigged. She's been on all night. Will you come?'

21　Night call

As I put down the phone I looked at the clock. It was two o'clock. I couldn't believe it. A job like that right on top of the champagne and smoked salmon. And right out in the wilds. It wasn't fair.

I took off my pyjamas and put on my shirt. As I put on the old trousers I used for work I tried not to look at the hired suit hanging up on the back of the door.

I found my way down the long garden to the garage. Beck Cottage was two miles away. It lay in a hollow. In the winter the place was a sea of mud. I slid through the mud all the way to the barn.

I went inside, past a row of cows and heaps of manure. Mr Atkinson did not believe in mucking out too often. I splashed my way through pools of urine to the end of the barn. I could just make out the shape of a pig on her side. There was a bed of straw under her. She lay very still, but now and again her flanks trembled. As I looked she held her breath and strained for a few seconds.

Mr Atkinson stood against a wall, one hand in his pocket. In the other he held a bike lamp. It looked as if the battery was running out.

'Is this all the light we've got?' I asked.

'Yes, it is,' said Mr Atkinson. He sounded surprised. His face had a 'what more does he want?' look.

'Let's have it, then,' I said, and trained the light on the pig. 'Just a young pig, isn't she?'

'Yes. Her first litter,' he said. The pig strained again, then lay still.

'Something is stuck, I think,' I said. 'Will you bring me a bucket of hot water, some soap and a towel, please?'

'Haven't got any hot water. The fire is out,' he replied.

'OK, bring me what you've got,' I said.

The farmer went off and then came back. He dumped a bucket of water on the floor. I dipped a finger in the water. It was ice cold.

Quickly I took off my jacket and shirt. The cold air made me gasp. I said through clenched teeth, 'Soap, please.'

'In the bucket,' he replied.

I put my arm into the water and felt my way round till I found the soap. I did my best to wash my hands with the hard soap. Then I knelt on the floor next to the pig.

Gently, I put my hand inside the pig. I moved my hand forward and had to roll over on my side. The stones were wet and cold. I forgot them, though, when my hand felt something. It was a little tail. A big piglet, I thought, stuck like a cork in a bottle.

With one finger I worked at the hind legs till I could grab them. I pulled the piglet out and said, 'This one's dead, I'm afraid. Been squashed too long. But there could be some live ones inside. I'll have another feel.'

I got down on the cold stones and put my hand in

again. Almost at arm's length I found another piglet. As I felt the face a set of very sharp teeth sank into my finger. I yelped.

'This one's alive, anyway. I'll soon have him out,' I said to the farmer.

I reached again and grasped one foot firmly between two fingers. I pulled the struggling piglet out into the world. Once out, the little piglet made its way round to its mother's teat.

'Poor old girl isn't helping at all,' I said. 'Been trying so long she's worn out. I'm going to give her an injection.'

I gave her a jab, and very soon the action of the drug started. Her womb began to squeeze the little piglets out. One after another eight piglets were born. The light from the lamp had almost given out by the time the after-birth came out of the pig.

I rubbed my cold arms. I felt chilled. I could not say how long I had stood there watching. I never grew tired of the wonder of birth.

Then I went to get dressed quickly. My right side was caked with dirt and muck. I did my best to scrape it off with my finger nails. Then I washed myself down with the cold water from the bucket.

'Have you got a towel there?' I asked. Mr Atkinson handed me a sack. It was stiff with manure. I took it and rubbed my chest with it. When I was dressed I climbed out of the pen. I had a last look before I left. The row of little pigs sucked away busily. Their mother gave a deep happy grunt.

I drove through the mud and up the hill. There I had to get out to open a gate. The wind with the cold clean smell of the frosty grass hit my face. I stood and looked across the dark fields. I thought of the night which was coming to an end. I thought of a careers talk I had heard at school.

Somebody had said, 'If you decide to become a vet you will never be rich, but you will have a life of endless interest and variety.'

I laughed out loud as I got into my car. He wasn't kidding. Variety. That was it – variety. Something different every hour of the day – and night.

22 Tristan baby-sits

The big black labrador lay on the table. His tongue
hung out and his eyes were shut. He had been brought
in with an ugly growth over his ribs. I had decided to
cut it out. Everything had turned out very well. I had
cut the growth out with no trouble at all. I felt sure it
would not come back. There was a tidy scar instead of
the ugly lump. I was pleased.

'Well, even if I say it myself, that looks good,' I said
to Tristan. Tristan looked at the stitches I had just put
into the cut I had made in the side of the dog.

'Very pretty indeed, my boy,' he said. 'Couldn't
have done better myself.'

'We had better keep him here till he comes round,'
I said. 'Give me a hand to get him on these blankets.'
We made the dog comfortable in front of an electric
stove. I left to start my morning round.

It was during lunch we first heard the strange sound.
It was something between a moan and a howl.

Siegfried looked up from his soup and said, 'What in
God's name is that?'

'Must be that dog I operated on this morning,' I
said. 'Now and again a dog does that when it is coming
round. I'm sure he'll stop soon.'

Siegfried looked at me and said, 'Well, I hope so. I could soon get tired of that noise. It gives me the creeps.'

We went and looked at the dog. His pulse was strong, his breathing was fine, and his colour was good. He was still deeply asleep, but he was still howling, about once every ten seconds.

'Yes, he's OK,' Siegfried said. 'But what a noise! Let's get out of here.'

The howling went on as we finished our lunch. As soon as he had finished eating Siegfried said, 'Well, I must fly. I've got a lot on this afternoon. Tristan, I think it would be a good idea to put the dog in the sitting-room. Put him by the fire. Then you can stay by him and keep your eye on him.'

Tristan was stunned and said, 'You mean I have to stay in the same room as that noise all afternoon?'

'Yes, that's what I mean,' Siegfried said. 'We can't send him home as he is. I don't want anything to happen to him. You must look after him.'

Tristan and I carried the heavy animal into the sitting-room. Then I had to go and start the afternoon round. I left quickly because the noise was so terrible.

It was dark when I got back. The house was quiet – except for the howling. I could hear it out in the street.

It was six o'clock. Tristan had had four hours of it. When I went into the sitting-room the noise seemed as if it would split my head. Tristan stood by the window with his back to me. I could see lumps of cotton wool sticking out of his ears.

I tapped him on the shoulder. He nearly jumped out of his skin.

'God help us, Jim, you nearly killed me,' he said.

'The only thing I can hear through these ear plugs is that dog.'

I got down and had a good look at the dog. He was in fine shape, but he did not seem to be coming round at all. And all the time there were the ear-splitting howls.

'He's taking a hell of a long time to come out of it,' I said. 'Has he been like this all afternoon?'

'Yes, just like that, the howling devil. He's as happy as a sandboy. Doesn't know a thing about it. But what about me? My nerves are shot to bits listening to him hour after hour. Much more of it and you'll have to give me a shot too,' said poor Tristan. He ran a shaking hand through his hair. I took his arm and led him into the dining-room.

'Come and eat. You'll feel better after some food,' I said.

Siegfried joined us and we ate our supper to the sound of the dog.

After supper, as we left the room, Siegfried said to me, 'Don't forget we've got to go to that vets' meeting tonight. It's a talk on the diseases of sheep. It should be good. Pity you can't come too, Tristan. I'm afraid you'll have to stay with the dog till he comes round.'

Tristan looked as if he'd been hit. 'Oh, not the evening as well with that dog! He's driving me mad!' he cried.

'I'm afraid so. James and I must go to this meeting. It would look bad if we didn't. Other-wise one of us could have taken over.'

Tristan stumbled back into the room. I put on my coat. As I went out into the street I stopped for a moment and listened. The dog was still howling.

23　A hard night

We enjoyed the meeting. The best part was the get-together of the vets in the bar afterwards. It was good to hear of other people's problems and mistakes. It made my own seem less bad. It was eleven o'clock before we all got into our cars and went home.

For a few hours I had quite forgotten poor Tristan. Still, I thought, the dog must be quiet by now. But, as I got out of my car I heard the howling. It was after midnight and the dog was still at it. And what about Tristan? I hated to think what kind of shape he'd be in. I felt quite scared as I went into the sitting-room.

Tristan's chair made a little island in a sea of empty beer bottles.

'Well, has it been rough, Triss? How do you feel now?' I asked.

'Could be worse, old lad, could be worse. Soon as you'd gone I went over to the pub for a crate of beer. It saved my life. After three or four I stopped worrying about the dog. As a matter of fact, I've been howling back at him for hours now. Anyway, he's coming round now. Look at him.'

The big dog had his head up and his eyes were open. The howling had stopped. I went over and patted him.

I said, 'That's better, old boy. But you'd better behave now. You've given Tristan one hell of a day.'

Siegfried came in. He told Tristan off about the mess of beer bottles in the room. He bent over and stroked the labrador's shiny head.

'Nice, friendly animal,' said Siegfried. 'I should think he's a grand dog when he's got his senses about him. He'll be fine in the morning. The problem is what to do about him now. We can't leave him down here, in case he staggers about and breaks a leg. Tristan, I think the best thing would be to take him up to your room tonight.'

'Thank you very much indeed,' said Tristan in a flat voice. I wondered what he was thinking.

Tristan's bedroom was next to mine. I helped Tristan up to his room. Then I carried the dog up. I laid the dog on a heap of blankets, in the corner of Tristan's bedroom.

'He's quiet now,' I said to Tristan. 'Sleeping like a baby. I'm sure he'll stay that way. You'll be able to have a rest.'

I went back into my own room, undressed and got into bed. I went to sleep right away. I couldn't tell you what time the noises started next door, but suddenly I was wide awake. An angry yell had woken me up. Then I heard a dragging noise and a bump, then another yell from Tristan.

I did not think it would be a good idea if I went in to Tristan. There was nothing I could do, anyway, so I lay still and listened. Every time I nearly fell asleep the bumping and shouting started again.

After about two hours the noises began to change. The labrador seemed to have control of his legs now.

He began marching up and down the room, his claws going tick, tick, tick on the floor. It went on and on.

Now and then I heard Tristan yelling, 'Stop it, for God's sake! Sit down, you stupid dog!'

I must have gone to sleep at last, because when I woke up it was morning. I listened. I could still hear a the tick, tick of the dog's claws, but it sounded as if the dog was strolling about, and not marching. There was no sound from Tristan.

I got dressed and quietly opened the door of Tristan's room. I almost fell over as two big feet were planted on my chest. The labrador was very pleased to see me.

'Well, you're all right, chum. Let's have a look at that scar.' It looked fine. 'Lovely!' I said. 'You're as good as new again.' He jumped up at me, licking my face.

I was fighting him off when I heard a groan from the bed. Tristan looked awful. He was grey, and his eyes were wild.

'Not a wink of sleep, Jim,' he said faintly. 'Not a wink. Wait till Siegfried hears about my night. It will really make his day. Just watch him. I bet you anything you like he looks pleased when I tell him about it.'

Later, over breakfast, Siegfried heard all about Tristan's night. He was full of sympathy, and said how sorry he was. But Tristan was right. He did look pleased.

24   A cold, wet morning

Vets get very used to dealing with the problem of milk fever in cows. It usually happens when a cow is giving milk. The cow gets weaker and weaker as she uses her strength to make milk.

This time, I was faced with a cow who had got milk fever soon after she had given birth to her calf, out of doors. She had then slipped down a muddy river bank. She was not conscious, and her back half was right under water. Her head rested on a shelf of rock. Her calf, wet and sad and in the early morning rain, was by her side, shaking.

Dan Cooper, her owner, looked worried as we made our way down to her.

'I think we're too late,' he said. 'She's dead, isn't she? I can't see her breathing.'

I replied, 'Pretty far gone, I'm afraid. If I can give her a shot of calcium she might come round.'

'I hope so. She's one of my best milkers. It always happens to the good ones,' groaned Dan.

He held some bottles of calcium for me, as I got a big needle into the syringe. It was early morning. My fingers were dead with cold. The water was deep enough to come over the top of my wellingtons. I bent down and pushed the needle into a vein at the base of the cow's neck. Then the calcium began to flow into the vein.

I stood there in the icy water, holding the bottle of calcium up in the air, my fingers still dripping blood. The rain was working its way inside my collar. I tried not to think of all the people I knew who were still in bed. Perhaps I should have been a doctor. They look after people in nice warm bedrooms.

The cow did not seem to be getting any better, so I injected the other bottle of calcium into her. It was then that I saw her eyelids move. I felt very pleased and said to Dan, 'She's still with us, Dan. We'll wait a few minutes, then roll her on to her chest.'

Within a quarter of an hour she began to toss her head about. I knew it was time to move her. I took hold of her horns and pulled. Dan and his son pushed at her shoulder. Slowly we got her on to her chest. Right away things looked much better. When a cow is lying on her side she always has the look of death on her.

I was pretty sure she would get better, but I could not go away and leave her lying there. I decided to stay a bit longer.

She did not like being in the water. She began to try to stand up. But it took her half an hour to get to her feet. Dan Cooper was very pleased. Using calcium on cows with milk fever was still a new idea then. I found it very thrilling to use it on a cow who might otherwise have died.

We helped the cow up the bank. At the top the full force of the wind hit us. We made our way towards the house. Dan and his son led, holding the calf in a sack between them.

We left the cow in a warm shed, giving her calf a

good lick. We took off our wellingtons in the porch. In the kitchen there was a good fire going and the smell of bacon cooking.

Mrs Cooper sent Dan and the boy up to change their wet socks, then she turned to me and said, 'All right, off with the socks, and your coat. Roll up your trousers and sit here.' She handed me a towel and told me to dry my hair. Then she filled a big bowl with hot water, and added some mustard.

'Here, stick your feet in this,' she said. I yelled as I put my feet in the bowl as it was hot, but Mrs Cooper took no notice. She just handed me a mug of hot tea.

By the time I had drunk half the tea I felt much better. Next she put in front of me a plate with two eggs, a big cut of bacon and four sausages. The bacon was home-cured, and the sausages were home-made. It was the first time I had eaten home-made Yorkshire sausage. They were wonderful, and Mrs Cooper was pleased that I enjoyed them so much.

I finished my breakfast, pulled on a pair of Dan's socks and my dry shoes. I was about to go when Mrs Cooper tucked a parcel under my arm. I knew it was some more of her sausages, so I thanked her very much.

I got home feeling warm, full of good food, and pleased that I had been able to save the cow.

25　A pig's ear

One morning I met Tristan in the garden, as I was going out to my car. He stopped me and showed me two tickets.

'Village dance tonight, Jim. It will be jolly good. Some of the nurses I know from the hospital are going. I'll see you are all right. And that's not all, look here.' He went into the saddle room and lifted up a loose board in the floor. He took out a bottle of sherry and said, 'We'll be able to have a good drink between dances.' I didn't ask where the sherry had come from.

That evening Tristan came out with me on my last call. In the car we talked about the dance. The case was easy – a cow with a bad eye. But the farm was high up in the hills, and by the time we had finished the job it was getting dark.

When we got back home Siegfried was out. There was a note for Tristan on the shelf in the sitting-room. It said,

'Tristan go home. S.'

This had happened before. When Siegfried invited people to stay he packed Tristan off home to his mother. Often Tristan did not mind, and would get on a train home quite happily. But not tonight.

'Good God, somebody must be coming for the night. Of course *I'm* the one who has to move out. It's a very nice carry on, I must say! And isn't that a charming letter! It doesn't matter if I don't want to. Oh no! Nobody asks me if I mind. It's just "Tristan, go home". Kind and polite, isn't it?'

He did not usually get worked up like this. I tried to calm him down.

'Look, Triss, perhaps we'd better skip this dance. There will be others,' I said.

Tristan clenched his fists and said, 'Why should I let him push me around like this? I have my own life to lead. I'm not going home tonight. I'm damn well going to the dance!'

This was fighting talk. I was worried. I said, 'Wait a minute. What about Siegfried? What's he going to say when he comes in and finds you still here?'

'To hell with Siegfried!' said Tristan. So I left it at that.

Siegfried came home when we were upstairs, changing. I was first down and found him sitting by the fire, reading. I said nothing but sat down and waited.

After a few moments Tristan came in. He looked smart in his best suit.

Siegfried looked up from his book and went red. 'What the hell are you doing here?' he said. 'I told you to go home. I've got a chap coming to stay tonight.'

'I couldn't go. There are no trains tonight,' said Tristan.

Siegfried sank back in his chair. I could see he was angry. He thought for a moment. Then he smiled.

'All right,' he said suddenly, 'Maybe, it's just as well you are staying. I want you to do a job for me. You can open that blood blister on Charlie Dent's pig's ear.'

This was a bombshell. Charlie Dent's pig's ear was something we did not talk about.

A few weeks before, Siegfried himself had gone along to see a pig with a bad ear at a small-holding on the edge of town. It was a blood blister. The only thing to do was to lance it – but for some reason Siegfried had not done the job. He sent me the next day.

I had wondered about it, but not for long. When I got into the sty the biggest sow I had ever seen rose from the straw. She rushed at me with her mouth open. I did not stop to argue. I reached the wall about six inches in front of the pig. I jumped over just in time. I stood there looking at the mean little red eyes, and the big mouth with its yellow teeth.

Usually I was not scared of pigs, but this one did seem to mean trouble. As I wondered what I should do next, the pig gave an angry roar. She got up on her hind legs and tried to get over the wall at me.

I made up my mind quickly, and said, 'I'm afraid I haven't got the right instrument with me, Mr Dent. I'll pop back in a day or so and open up that ear for you. Don't worry, it's only a small job. Good-bye.'

Nobody had said anything about it since.

Tristan looked very upset. 'You mean you want me to go along there tonight? But I'm going to a dance,' he said.

Siegfried smiled and said, 'It has to be done now. That's an order. You can go to your dance afterwards.'

Tristan started to say something, but he knew he had pushed his luck far enough.

'Right,' he said. 'I'll go and do it.'

He left the room. Siegfried went back to reading his

book. I stared into the fire, wondering how Tristan would handle this one.

Within ten minutes he was back.

'Have you opened that ear?' Siegfried asked Tristan.

'No, I couldn't find the place. You must have given me the wrong address. Number 98 you said,' replied Tristan.

'It's number 89, and you know damn well it is. Now get back there and do the job,' said Siegfried.

Off went Tristan and again I waited. Quarter of an hour later in came Tristan, looking pleased.

Siegfried looked up from his book and asked, 'Have you done it?'

'No. The family are all out at the pictures,' said Tristan.

Siegfried looked as if he was going to explode. He said, 'I don't care where the family are. Just get into that sty and lance that ear.'

Again Tristan set off and again we waited. Twenty minutes passed and Tristan was with us again. Siegfried said, 'Have you opened that ear?'

'No. It's pitch dark in there. How can I work? I've only got two hands – one for the knife and one for the torch. How can I hold the ear?'

Siegfried had been keeping a tight hold on himself, but now he lost his temper.

'Don't give me any more of your excuses,' he said, jumping out of his chair. 'I don't care how you do it, but by God, you are going to open that pig's ear to-night! Now get the hell out of here and don't come back till it's done!'

26 Tristan wins through

My heart bled for Tristan. He had tried everything. He had no more tricks left now. He stood at the door for a few moments. Then he turned and walked out.

The next hour was a long one. Siegfried seemed happy with his book. I tried to read too. I had just decided to go out for a walk, when Tristan came in.

In came a strong smell of pigs, too. Tristan's best suit was covered with pig's muck, so were his collar and face and hair. There was a great lump of the stuff on his trousers, but he did not seem to care. Siegfried moved his chair back quickly, because of the smell.

'Have you got that ear opened?' he asked quietly.

'Yes,' said Tristan. Siegfried went back to his book. Tristan turned and marched from the room. But even after he had gone the smell of pigs hung in the room like a cloud.

Later in the pub I watched Tristan drink his third pint. He had changed his suit, but he did not look as good as he had at the start of the evening. At least he was clean now, and hardly smelt at all. I went over to the bar and ordered my second half and Tristan's fourth pint. As I set the glasses on the table I thought perhaps it was time to ask what had happened.

Tristan took a long drink of his beer and lit a

cigarette. He said, 'Well now, Jim, all in all it was quite an easy job. I'll start at the beginning. I stood all alone outside the sty. I could hear that damn pig grunting on the other side of the wall. I didn't feel so good, I can tell you.'

'I shone my torch on the thing's face. It jumped up and ran at me. It roared at me and showed all those dirty yellow teeth. I nearly gave up and came home there and then. But I thought about the dance and, on the spur of the moment, I hopped over the wall.'

'Two seconds later I was on my back. It must have charged me, but it couldn't see well enough to bite me.'

'Well, it's a funny thing, Jim. You know I'm not a rough chap, but as I lay there, I wasn't scared any more. I just hated that damn animal. Before I knew what I was doing I was on my feet, booting its behind. I kicked it round and round the sty. And, do you know, it showed no fight at all. That pig was a coward at heart.'

'But what about the ear?' I asked.

'No problem, Jim,' said Tristan, 'that was done for me. I was really very lucky. In the dark the pig ran up against the wall and burst the thing itself. Made a beautiful job.'

27 A giant problem

Spring had come. My first spring in Darrowby. It was not a warm spring, but it was dry. Sharp winds tossed the heads of the clumps of daffodils on the village greens. In April the roadside banks were bright with the fresh yellow of the primroses.

One morning Siegfried called to me as he was going out. 'James, there's a horse with a growth on its belly at Wilkinson's of White Cross. Get along there and take it off. Today, if you can. I'll leave it to you.'

Now, to tell the truth, I was no horseman. In fact I was scared of big horses. I really only liked them small – the smaller the better.

I boiled up my instruments with a heavy heart. I drove off to the farm with them rattling in a tray behind me. At Wilkinson's all was quiet. The yard was empty, except for a boy of about ten. He told me that he did not know where the boss was.

'Well, where is the horse?' I asked. The lad pointed to the stable.

'He's in there.'

I went inside. At the end stood a high loose-box From it I heard snorting, then a lot of very loud thuds against the sides of the box. A chill crept through me. That was no little colt in there.

I opened the top half of the door. There, looking down at me was a huge horse. I didn't know horses ever came as big as that. He had feet like man-hole covers. When he saw me he laid back his ears and showed the whites of his eyes. He lashed out at the side of the box with his foot. A foot long splinter of wood flew high in the air as the great hoof crashed down.

'God almighty,' I gasped as I closed the half door quickly. I leaned against the door and listened to my heart thumping. I asked the boy how old the horse was. He told me he was six.

I tried to think calmly. How did you get near a man-eater like this? I had never seen such a horse. I shook myself. I had not looked at the growth I was here to take off. I opened the door about two inches and peeped inside. I could see it clearly on the horse's belly. It was about the size of a cricket ball. It looked like a little cauliflower. It swung from side to side as the horse moved.

No trouble to take it off. Nice narrow neck to it. I could twist it off easily. But the snag was, how was I going to get to it?

I went and had a cup of tea with Mr and Mrs Wilkinson in the farm kitchen, while some of the men got a halter on the horse. Even from there we could hear the clatter the horse was making.

As we walked towards the stable I felt my mouth going dry. The noise was getting louder. Then the stable doors flew open and the great horse shot out into the yard. He was dragging two big men on the end of the halter rope. They had a hard time trying to get him to stay still. I could feel the ground shake as the hooves crashed down.

At last the men got the horse standing against the wall of the barn. When they both had hold of him firmly they said to me:

'Ready for you now, sir.'

I got the syringe ready to give the horse a shot to freeze the place where the growth was. My hands were trembling.

I walked up to the horse as if in a dream. I raised my left hand and took hold of the growth. I pulled it gently down, stretching the brown skin joining the growth to the belly of the horse.

I took a long breath, then put the needle of the syringe against the skin and pushed it in.

The kick was so quick that I just felt surprised that a big animal could move so fast. I did not even see the hoof coming. It struck my right leg and I spun round, helpless. When I hit the ground I lay still. Then I tried to move and a stab of pain went through my leg.

When I opened my eyes Mr Wilkinson was bending over me.

'Are you all right, Mr Herriot?' he asked.

I said, 'I don't think so. You'd better put the horse back in the box for now. We'll have a go another day. I wonder if you would ring Mr Farnon and ask him to pick me up? I don't think I shall be able to drive.'

My leg wasn't broken, just very badly bruised. I was still walking with a stick two weeks later, when Siegfried and I and an army of helpers went back to

Mr Wilkinson's place. We roped the horse, put him out with chloroform, and cut off the growth.

Some good came out of all this. I found out that fear can be worse than reality. Horses have never worried me quite so much since.

28   A dose of salts

Looking at Phin Calvert you would never have thought
that he was a rich farmer. He was a stumpy, thickset
little man. He wore a ragged jacket most of the time,
and he tucked his hands behind his braces. He wore
a shirt without a collar and a greasy old cap. He always
had a big smile on his face, and he hummed to himself
all the time. He did not look well off at all.

So I had a surprise when I was called to his place one
morning. I found a large, rather grand-looking house
and buildings. A fine dairy herd was grazing in the
fields.

I could hear him before I got out of the car.

'Hello, hello, hello, who's this we've got, then? A
new chap, then? Now we're going to learn something!'
he said. He had his hands inside his braces and a wide
grin on his face.

'My name's Herriot,' I said.

'Is it now?' he said, looking me over. He turned to
three young men standing by and said to them,
'Hasn't he a nice smile, lads? He's a real Happy
Harry!'

He led the way across the yard, saying to me,

'Come and show us what you're made of. I hope you

know a bit about calves. I've got some here that are a bit odd.'

As we went into the calf house I hoped I would be able to do something to show them how good I was. Perhaps I could use some of the very new drugs that I had in my car. It would take something good to make my mark with these people.

There were six well-grown animals in the calf house. Three of them were acting very strangely. They ground their teeth and frothed at the mouth. They were moving about as if they could not see. As I watched, one of them walked right into the wall and stood with its nose pressed against the stone. Phin watched me as I got hold of one of the animals and took its temperature. Phin was still humming to himself.

Usually while I'm taking an animal's temperature I'm thinking hard. But this time I did not need time to decide what was the matter. The blindness made it easy. I began to look round the walls of the calf house. It was dark so I had to get my face close to the stone.

Phin said in a surprised voice, 'Hey, what's going on? You're as bad as the calves nosing about there. What do you think you're looking for?'

I replied, 'Paint, Mr Calvert. I think your calves have got lead poisoning.'

Phin said what all farmers say at this moment:

'They can't have. I've had calves in here for thirty years and they've never come to any harm before. There's no paint in here, anyway.'

'How about this then?' I said. In the darkest corner was a loose board. I pulled it out.

'Oh, that's only a bit of wood I put down there last

week to block up a hole. It came off an old hen house,' he said.

I looked at the old paint hanging off in flakes. Calves love the taste of this.

'This is what's done the damage,' I said. 'Look, you can see the tooth marks where they've been at it.'

'All right,' Phin said. 'What do we do now?'

'First thing is to get this painted wood out of here. Then we give all the calves Epsom salts. Have you got any?' I asked.

Phin laughed and said, 'I've got a huge great sack full. But can't you do better than that? Aren't you going to inject them or something?'

I felt embarrassed. At that time the new drugs to cure lead poisoning had not been found. The only thing that sometimes did a bit of good was Epsom salts.

'No,' I said. 'The only thing that will help at all is Epsom salts, and I don't know if that will work. I'd like you to give the calves two heaped tablespoonfuls three times a day.'

'Oh hell,' he said, 'you'll give the poor things the runs until they die!'

'Maybe so, but there's nothing else for it,' I said.

Phin took a step towards me. His face was close to mine. He looked at me steadily. Then he turned away quickly and said, 'Right. Come in and have a drink.' We all went over to the farm kitchen together. As we went in Phin shouted so loud the windows shook.

'Mother! Come and meet Happy Harry! We all want a glass of beer!'

Mrs Calvert quickly came in and put out glasses and bottles. I filled my glass. It was the first of many good beers I was to drink at that table.

Mrs Calvert smiled at me and said, 'Can you do anything for the calves, then?'

Before I could answer Phin said, 'He's put them on Epsom salts. I said when he came we would get something real smart and scientific. You can't beat new blood and modern ideas.' Phin drank his beer with a very straight face.

In the following days the calves got better. At the end of a fortnight they were all eating normally, thank goodness.

29 Mr Calvert again

It was not long before I saw Phin again. It was early afternoon. I was in the office with Siegfried. I heard someone come to the door humming to himself.

'Well, well, well,' he shouted at Miss Harbottle, 'it's Flossie! And what's my little darling doing today?'

Miss Harbottle's face did not change. She gave Phin an icy stare, but then Phin saw Siegfried. 'How's tricks?' he asked him.

'Everything's fine, Mr Calvert,' Siegfried replied. 'What can we do for you?'

Phin pointed at me and said, 'There's my man. I want him out at my place right sharp.'

'What's the trouble?' I asked. 'Is it the calves again?'

'Damn, no! I wish it was. It's my good bull. He's puffing like an engine. Bit like a bad cold, but worse than I've known. He's in a hell of a state. Looks like he's dying.' For a moment Phin did not look so pleased with life.

I had heard of this bull. It was a show winner, the pride of his herd.

'I'll be right with you, Mr Calvert,' I said.

'Good lad, I'm off then.' He stopped at the door and gave Miss Harbottle a wicked smile. 'Ta-ta, Flossie!' he cried, and was gone.

For a moment the room seemed very quiet, apart from Miss Harbottle saying, 'Oh, that man! Dreadful, dreadful!'

I made it in good time to the farm. Phin was waiting for me, and his three sons. The sons looked gloomy, but Phin looked cheerful enough.

'Here he is!' he shouted. 'Here's Happy Harry! Now we'll be all right again.' He hummed to himself as we walked over to the bull pen, but when he looked over the door he stopped.

The bull was standing in the middle of the pen. I had never seen an animal finding it so hard to breathe. His ribs rose and fell, his mouth hung open. Foam covered his lips and nose. His eyes, wide with fear, stared at the wall in front of him. This was not a bad cold. It was a fight for breath. It looked as if the fight was lost, too.

He did not move as I took his temperature. I thought very hard. I had expected fast breathing, but nothing like this.

'Poor old beggar,' Phin said. 'He's bred me the finest calves I've ever had. He's as quiet as a sheep, too. I hate to see him suffer like this. If you can't do any good, just tell me and I'll get the gun out.'

I read the bull's temperature. One hundred and ten degrees! This was mad. I thought I'd better try again. I gave it nearly a minute this time, so that I could do some extra thinking. Again I read one hundred and ten degrees.

What in the name of God was this? I thought and thought. I had no answer. I looked at the people watching me. I looked out of the window at the sunshine. Sunshine. A faint bell rang in my mind.

'Has he been out today?' I asked.

'Yes, he's been out on the grass all morning. It was that grand and warm,' said Phin. The bell rang loudly in my mind, and suddenly I knew the answer.

'Get a hosepipe in here quick,' I said. 'He's got sunstroke.'

They had the hose fixed in less than a minute. I turned it full on. I played the jet of cold water all over the huge body; his face and neck, his ribs and up and down his legs. I kept this up for about five minutes. It seemed longer as I waited for something to happen. I began to think I was on the wrong track, when the bull gulped just once.

It was something. The bull had not been able to swallow at all before. I began to see a change in the animal. He did not look quite so sad. His breathing began to slow down a bit. Then the bull shook himself. He turned his head and looked at us.

'By God, it's working!' said one of the sons.

I enjoyed myself after that. I cannot think of anything in my work that has pleased me more than saving that bull.

'He'll be all right now,' I said. 'I must go now, but I think one of the lads should keep the water on him for another twenty minutes.'

'You've time for a drink,' Phin said.

In the farm kitchen we drank beer again. From his armchair Phin said, 'Happy Harry, I'm lost for words. I don't know what to say to you.'

It was not often that Phin lost his voice. But he found it again very soon at the next farmers' meeting.

A speaker had just been telling us about all the latest ideas and newest drugs.

It was too much for Phin. He jumped to his feet and cried, 'I think you are talking rubbish. There's a young fellow in Darrowby who has only just left college. He uses nothing but Epsom salts and cold water, whatever you call him out for.'

30   One in the eye for Siegfried

Now and again Siegfried would decide to turn over a
new leaf. Everyone suffered when he had these spells.
They usually came after he had been reading the latest
scientific books, or when he had seen a film about the
newest methods for vets. He would rush around telling
both Tristan and me to be better men. For a time
nothing was good enough, unless it was perfect.

He would make our life hell. He would say things
like, 'We must put on a better show when we go to
these farms. It isn't good enough to fish out a few old
instruments from a bag and start hacking at the
animal. Everything must be clean and spotless. Our
work must be perfect.'

So Siegfried was very pleased when a cow that
belonged to a friend of his needed an operation. It had
picked up a bit of wire that had got stuck in its second
stomach. So Siegfried was going to cut open Colonel
Merrick's cow and take out the wire.

'We'll show Hubert a thing or two. We'll give him
a show of skill that he'll never forget,' Siegfried said.

Tristan and I were going along to help. Siegfried
led the way to the farm. He looked extra smart in a
brand new jacket that he was very proud of. He shook
hands with his friend, the Colonel.

'I hear you are going to operate on my cow,' Colonel Merrick said. 'I'd like to watch you do it, if it's all right with you.'

'By all means, Hubert, please do. You'll find it very interesting,' Siegfried said with a smile.

In the cow-shed Tristan and I had to rush around. We set tables along-side the cow. On these we put new metal trays with rows of shining instruments.

Siegfried fussed around as happy as a school boy. He had clever hands and with a knife in them he was worth watching. I could read his mind without much trouble. This, he was thinking, was going to be good.

When he had everything the way he wanted it, he took off his new jacket. He put on a shining white smock. He handed the jacket to Tristan.

Suddenly he roared with anger: 'Don't throw it down like that! Here, give it to me. I'll find a safe place for it.' He dusted the new jacket down, and hung it on a nail on the wall.

I had already shaved and cleaned the place where Siegfried was going to open up the animal. Everything was ready to give the animal an injection so that it did not feel any pain. As Siegfried injected he said to his friend:

'This is where we go inside, Hubert. I hope you've got a strong stomach.' The Colonel smiled. 'Oh, I've seen blood before. You needn't worry, I shan't faint.'

With a bold stroke Siegfried cut into the animal. Now we could all see the wall of the first stomach.

Siegfried picked up a fresh knife. He looked for the best place to cut in. But as he stood with his knife ready, the wall of the first stomach bulged out through the first cut.

'Funny,' Siegfried muttered, 'must be some gas in there.'

He was not worried, he just pushed the bulge back in through the cut. He got ready to make another cut. But as he took his hand away, the stomach wall bulged out again. This time it was bigger than a football.

Siegfried pushed it back again – and it shot out again, right away. This time he took two hands to the job. He pushed and pushed till he pushed the bulge once more back inside. He stood out of breath for a moment with his hands inside the cow. He was sweating.

He took his hands away. Nothing happened. It must have stopped. He went to pick up the knife, when, like a live thing, out came the bulge again. It was huge.

Siegfried stopped pretending nothing was wrong. He started to fight, both arms round the thing, pushing it back with all his strength. I went to help him. Silently we fought the mass till it had gone inside again. The Colonel was watching carefully. He had not thought the operation would be so interesting.

'It must be the gas that's doing it,' said Siegfried. 'Pass me the knife and stand back, James.'

He stuck the knife into the stomach wall and made a cut. I was glad I had moved away. Through the opening shot a jet of all that was in the stomach, a greenish-brown stinking mess.

The first direct hit was on Siegfried's face. He could not let go of the stomach in case it went back inside the animal, and filled it with muck. So he hung on to each side of the opening, while the mess poured out on to his hair, down his neck and all over his white smock.

Now and then the steady stream of muck would

suddenly come out in a gush which spread over everything in range. Within a minute the trays and the shining instruments were covered. The worst happened when a very strong jet shot over Siegfried's beautiful new jacket.

The Colonel's mouth hung open in surprise at the sight. Siegfried hung on grimly. We could not see his face any more, but we could guess how he was feeling.

At last the flood slowed down and stopped. I was able to hold the sides of the opening so that Siegfried could put his hand inside the animal for the bit of wire.

Tristan had been busy washing the things Siegfried needed to stitch up the cut. Soon the whole job was over. Everything looked fine. The cow did not seem at all worried. She knew and felt nothing of Siegfried's struggle with her insides.

It took quite a time to tidy up the mess. The hardest part was trying to clean Siegfried up. We did our best to wash him down with buckets of water. All the time he scraped sadly at his new jacket with a flat stick.

The Colonel was full of praise for Siegfried. He said, 'Come in for a drink, my dear chap,' but he took care to stand at least ten feet away from his friend. Siegfried thanked him, but said we must be off.

On the way home in the car Tristan and I could not get as far away from Siegfried as we should have liked. Even with our heads stuck out of the windows the smell was still pretty bad.

Siegfried drove for a mile or two and then he turned to me and grinned.

'You never know what's round the corner in this game, boys,' he said. Really, nothing got him down for long.

31 Mr Cranford

Isaac Cranford was a hard man. He struck a hard bargain. In a part of the world where everybody was careful with their money, he was noted for his meanness. He farmed some of the best land in the Dales. His cattle often won prizes at shows, but he was nobody's friend. He was a man who had to win at all costs. People said about him 'If he gets his hand on a pound note, by God, it's a prisoner.'

One afternoon I had a phone call from him. He said, 'I've a cow struck by lightning. She's laid dead in the field.' I was surprised.

'Lightning?' I said, 'are you sure? We haven't had a storm today.'

'Maybe you haven't, but we have here,' he replied.

'Mmm, all right, I'll come and have a look at her,' I said.

So next morning I drove to the farm. I was not looking forward to seeing Mr Cranford. This lightning business could be a bit of a headache. All farmers were insured against lightning. After a bad thunder storm it was quite usual for the vets' phones to start ringing. Farmers wanted them to come and look at dead animals.

The insurance firms understood this. If the vet told

them that he thought that an animal had been killed by lightning, they paid up without a fuss. In cases of doubt they would ask another vet if he agreed. The trouble was there were no real signs of the cause of death on an animal killed by lightning. Sometimes there was a bruise under the skin, but very little else. It was easy when the animal had scorch marks running from an ear down the leg to the ground. Often the animal would be found under a tree which had been struck by lightning.

Most farmers only looked for a fair deal. If their vet found some other clear cause of death they would take his word for it. But the odd one could be difficult.

I had a feeling that Mr Cranford might well be difficult. He was in the habit of getting his own way, right or wrong. If he did not get it today there would be trouble.

He was standing still in the middle of the farmyard. He nodded at me, then led the way to a field at the back of the house.

The dead cow lay in the middle of the field. There were no trees anywhere near the cow. We stopped beside the cow. Mr Cranford was the first to speak.

'Must be lightning. Can't be anything else. Nasty storm, then this good cow dropped dead.'

I looked at the grass around the cow. It was all churned up and torn out. I said:

'It hasn't just dropped down, has it? It died in a fit. You can see where its feet kicked out the grass.'

'All right then, it had a fit, but it was the lightning that did it.' Mr Cranford's angry little eyes looked at my collar, my belt, my wellingtons. He could never bring himself to look anyone right in the eye.

'I don't think so, Mr Cranford,' I said. 'One of the signs of lightning killing an animal is that it has fallen without a struggle. Some of them even have grass in their mouths.'

'Oh, I know all about that,' snapped Cranford. 'This isn't the first cow I've seen struck by lightning. They are not all the same you know.'

'Yes, but you see this death could have been caused by a lot of things. I think we ought to open it up to make sure,' I said.

'Now see here, are you saying I'm trying to do something I shouldn't?' Mr Cranford said.

'Not at all,' I replied. 'I'm only saying I should like to be sure. We can go and see her opened up at the knacker's yard. If there's no sign of anything else wrong, you'll have the benefit of the doubt. The insurance people are pretty good about it.'

Mr Cranford looked very angry. His little eyes flashed.

'I've had vets at these jobs before. Vets who really knew what they were doing. They've never messed about like this. What's the use of going to all that trouble?'

Why indeed, I thought. Why make an enemy of this man? He was rich and knew a lot about farming. If people did not like him, they still listened to him. He could do a young vet a lot of harm. Perhaps it was lightning anyway.

I turned to face Mr Cranford. I tried to look into his eyes, but he always looked away.

'I'm sorry,' I said, 'but I think we really ought to have a look inside this cow. I'll meet you at the knacker's yard in the morning at ten o'clock. Will that be all right?'

'Suppose it will have to be,' spat out Cranford. 'All nonsense. Let me remind you – this was a good cow. I can't afford to lose money. I want my rights.'

'I'm sure you'll get them, Mr Cranford. Before I have her moved I'd better do a blood test on her, to see if her blood was all right.'

He left me to it. He was too angry to speak to me again that morning.

It was not a very happy meeting next morning at the knacker's yard. Bending over the dead cow I could not find a clue as to what killed it. There was no sign of a bruise when the skin came off. The organs inside the body looked quite clean and normal. I asked the owner of the yard to cut into the heart.

He sliced that big organ from top to bottom. Right away I knew my search was over. The heart was in a very poor state. It was almost full up with a growth that looked like a cauliflower.

'That's what killed your cow, Mr Cranford,' I said.

'Rubbish!' Cranford yelled. 'You're not telling me that little thing could kill a beast like that.'

'Not so little, I'm afraid. You can see for yourself,' I replied. Then he turned to me and tried to smile. It was a dreadful sight. For one awful moment his eyes met mine.

He drew me to one side and said, 'Mr Herriot, we're both men of the world. You know as well as I do that the insurance can afford to lose this money more than I can. Why can't we just say it's lightning?'

'But what would bother me, Mr Cranford, is that I should know that it *wasn't* lightning,' I said. 'It's no good. I can't say that cow was struck by lightning, and that's that.'

Mr Cranford went deep red with anger. His voice shook as he said to me:

'Well, I'll tell you this, I'm going to see your boss about you. You don't know your job! You'll hear more of this. I'll tell you one thing, you'll never walk on my farm again!' He turned and hurried away. I got into my car. Well, everything had worked out just great. If only I could stick to treating sick animals! But there were so many other things to worry about as well. I drove away.

32   Mr Cranford complains

It did not take Mr Cranford long to do as he had
threatened. The next day he came to the house soon
after lunch. Siegfried and I were sitting having a
cigarette when we heard the door bell. We did not get
up, as most of the farmers walked in after ringing.

The dogs went mad as usual. They jumped up from
the rug in front of the fire and rushed out into the
passage.

People often wondered why Siegfried kept five dogs.
Not only kept them but took them everywhere with
him. When he drove his car on his rounds it was hard
to see him at all among the waving tails and shaggy
heads. Anybody going near the car would be scared
out of their life by the loud barking, glaring eyes and
sharp teeth they could see through the car window.

'I don't know why people keep dogs as pets,' Siegfried often said. 'A dog should be useful. It should be
used for farm work, for shooting, or as a guide. Why
anybody should keep them just for hanging round the
place beats me.'

He would often say this sort of thing as he sat in his
car, dogs all round him. The person listening to him
would look in surprise at the dogs. There was a grey-
hound, a tiny terrier, a spaniel, a whippet and a scottie.

Nobody every asked Siegfried why he kept his own dogs.

I think Siegfried's dogs fell upon Mr Cranford in the passage. Some people would have fled, but I could hear him fighting his way in. When he came to the sitting-room he had taken off his hat. He was beating the dogs off with it. The man's eyes stared, and his lips were moving, but we could not hear anything.

Siegfried, always polite, got up and pointed to a chair. Mr Cranford sat down. The dogs sat in a ring round him, barking up into his face. They did not like Mr Cranford.

Mr Cranford kept on talking. Siegfried sat and seemed to be listening. Almost nothing could be heard from Mr Cranford. The dogs went on barking. Sometimes a word or two came over.

'. . . want to complain. . . .'
'. . . doesn't know his job. . . .'
'. . . can't afford. . . . not a rich man. . . .'
'. . . these damn dogs. . . .'
'. . . won't have him again. . . .'
'. . . down, dog, down. . . .'
'. . . not going to be robbed. . . .'

Siegfried listened. As the time passed I could see that the strain was beginning to tell on Mr Cranford. His eyes began to glare and the veins stood out on his thin neck. At last he gave up. He jumped up and made his way to the door. The dogs went with him. He shouted with rage, lashed out at them again with his hat, and was gone.

33 A terrible muddle

As I went into the dispensary a few weeks later I found my boss mixing an ointment. He was working with great care.

'What's this you're doing?' I asked.

'Ointment for a boar,' he said. He looked past me at Tristan who had just come in. 'And I don't know why the hell I'm doing it when some people are sitting around on their backsides.' He pointed to the ointment. 'Right, Tristan, you have a go. When you've finished your cigarette, that is.'

He turned to me and said, 'The ointment is for your old friend Cranford. For that prize boar of his. It's got a nasty sore across its back and he's worried to death about it. It wins him a lot of money at the shows. A sore there could lose the prizes for him.'

'Cranford is still with us then,' I said.

'Yes,' said Siegfried. 'It's a funny thing, we can't get rid of him. I don't like losing custom, but I'd gladly lose him. He won't have you near the place after that lightning job. He doesn't think much of me either. He gives me the creeps. But he won't find himself another vet. He damn well won't leave us.'

'He knows which side his bread is buttered,' I said. 'He gets first rate service from us.'

Siegfried smiled and said, 'I wish there was a simple way to get rid of him.' He tapped Tristan on the shoulder and said, 'That'll do. Don't strain yourself. Put it in a box and write on it, "Rub well into the boar's back three times a day. Work it well in with the fingers." Then post it to Mr Cranford. And after you've done that, will you post this dung sample to the lab, to have it tested for disease.' He held out a treacle tin brimming with stinking, watery dung.

It was quite usual to send samples like this for testing for worms, and other diseases. The samples were always very large. Really, only a very small amount was needed for the tests. But the farmers always sent masses and masses. 'Take plenty, we've lots of it,' they said.

Tristan took hold of the tin very carefully. He began to look on the shelves. He said:

'We don't seem to have any of those little glass sample jars.'

'That's right. We're out of them,' said Siegfried. 'I meant to order some more. But never mind, put the lid on that tin and press it down hard. Then wrap it up in brown paper. It will get to the lab all right.'

It took only three days for Mr Cranford's name to come up again. Siegfried sat opening the morning post. Suddenly he sat very still. He froze as he read a letter.

Then he looked up and said, 'James, this is the strongest letter I have ever had. It's from Cranford. He's finished with us for good. What's more, he is thinking of taking us to court.'

'What have we done this time?' I asked.

'He says we have insulted him, and put his boar in danger. He says we sent him a tin of cow dung and told him to rub it on the boar's back three times a day.'

Tristan got up quickly and walked towards the door. Siegfried shouted at him: 'Tristan! Come back here! Sit down, we've got something to talk about.'

He went on as Tristan sat down, 'So you've done it again. I can't trust you to do anything. It wasn't much to ask was it? Two little parcels to post. You muddled them up didn't you?'

Tristan started to say he was sorry, but Siegfried went on, 'Oh, don't worry. Your usual good luck has saved you again. With anybody else but Cranford it would have been an awful mistake. But I'm only too pleased to get rid of him.' He stopped for a moment and then said with a smile, 'The label said to work well in with the fingers, I remember. Mr Cranford said he opened the parcel at the breakfast table. . . .'

'But what about the law business?' I said.

'Oh, I think we can forget about that. Mr Cranford won't want to look a fool. Just think how it would sound in court,' said Siegfried. 'There's another thing, of course. I wonder how the lab is making out, testing that ointment?'

34   A cure for Tricki Woo

I was really worried about Tricki this time. I had
stopped the car in the street to talk to Mrs Pumfrey.
I was shocked when I saw him. He was now so fat that
he looked like a sausage with a leg at each corner. His
eyes were bloodshot and his tongue lolled out of his
mouth.

When she saw me looking at him Mrs Pumfrey said,
'He was so lifeless I thought he wasn't getting enough
food, so I have been giving him a few extras to build
him up.'

'And did you cut down on the sweet things as I told
you?' I asked sternly.

'Oh, I did for a bit, but he seemed so weak,' she
said. 'I had to give way. He does love his cream cakes
and his biscuits so. I can't say no to him.'

I looked down at the little dog. That was the
trouble. Tricki was so greedy. He would eat at any
time of the night or day.

'Now I really mean this. If you don't cut his food
right down he is going to be very ill,' I said.

'Oh, I will, Mr Herriot, I will,' said Mrs Pumfrey,
and she set off down the road, back to the car.

I watched them. Tricki tottered along in his little

tweed coat. I thought it would not be long before I heard from Mrs Pumfrey.

The call came within a few days. She was beside herself with worry. Tricki would eat nothing. He was being sick often. He spent all his time lying on a rug panting. He did not want to do anything.

I had already decided what to do. I had to get Tricki out of that house for a time. My idea was that he should be put in hospital for at least two weeks.

Poor Mrs Pumfrey almost fainted. They had never been apart before. She was sure he would pine and die if he did not see her every day.

But I took a firm line. Tricki was very ill and this was the only way to save him. In fact, I thought it best to take him there and then. I marched out to the car carrying the little dog.

All the servants rushed in and out of the house with his day bed, his night bed, his cushions, toys and rubber rings, breakfast bowl, lunch bowl, supper bowl. As I drove away I looked in the mirror. Everybody was in tears.

Out on the road I looked down at Tricki. I patted his head. Bravely he tried to wag his tail.

At home, all Siegfried's dogs came to see him. Tricki looked at them with dull eyes. When I put him down he just lay on the carpet. The other dogs sniffed him. They decided he was not very interesting, so they left him alone.

I made up a bed for him near where the other dogs slept in the stables. For two days I kept an eye on him. I gave him no food, but lots of water. At the end of the second day he started to show some interest in what was going on. On the third day he seemed to want to go out when he heard the other dogs in the yard.

When I opened the door Tricki trotted out. Straight away the dogs rushed towards him. After rolling him over and having a good look, the dogs moved down the garden. Tricki followed them.

Later that day I watched the dogs at feeding time. There was the usual rush followed by high speed eating.

When they had finished Tricki walked round the shining bowls. He gave a lick at one or two of them. Next day an extra bowl was put down for him.

From then on he got better very quickly. He had no medicine of any kind, but all day he ran around with the dogs. He was bowled over, trampled on and squashed every few minutes. He was very happy. He became a member of the gang. He fought for his share of food at meal times, and hunted for rats in the old hen house at night. He had never had such a time in his life.

35   Tricki Woo goes home

All the time Mrs Pumfrey stayed in touch. She rang at least a dozen times a day for news of Tricki. I told her Tricki was out of danger, and on the mend.

At this she started to send round fresh eggs, two dozen at a time. These were to build up Tricki's strength. We had two eggs each for breakfast from then on. Then bottles of sherry started to arrive.

These were for Tricki's blood. We had two glasses before lunch, and several during the meal. We took turns to toast Tricki's health.

We could hardly believe it when the brandy came. Siegfried dug out some balloon glasses. For a few evenings they were in constant use.

They were very happy days. We started with the extra egg in the morning. We had our sherry at noon and finished the evening round the fire with brandy.

I was tempted to have Tricki with us for keeps, but I knew how Mrs Pumfrey was suffering. After a fortnight I phoned her to tell her that the little dog was quite fit and that she could come and get him.

Within minutes her car drew up outside. I went to speak to her.

'Oh, Mr Herriot, do tell me the truth,' she said. 'Is he really better?'

'Yes, he's fine. There's no need for you to get out of the car. I'll go and get him for you.'

I walked through the house into the garden. A mass of dogs was running round and round the garden. In the middle was Tricki, ears flapping, tail wagging. In two weeks he had changed into a trim, slim, fit animal. He was keeping up with the gang.

I carried him back to the car. When Tricki saw Mrs Pumfrey he took off from my arms in a great jump into her lap.

While Tricki was barking and licking Mrs Pumfrey, all his beds, toys, cushions, coats and bowls were put in the car. None of them had been used. As the car moved away she leaned out of the car window. Tears shone in her eyes.

'Oh, Mr Herriot, how can I ever thank you? This is a miracle of science!'

36 Giving a hand

I woke up with a jump. The phone was ringing. The voice on the other end of the phone sounded wide awake and cheerful.

'I have a mare foaling. She doesn't seem to be getting on with the job. Can you come and give me a hand?'

This was just a bit too much. Out of bed in the middle of the night was bad enough, but twice was sheer cruelty. I had had a hard day. I had been glad to get to bed at midnight. I had had to get out at one o'clock to help a calf to be born. I had not got back to bed till three. What was the time now? Three fifteen. Good God, I had only had a few minutes' sleep. What a life!

'Right, Mr Dixon, I'll come straight away,' I said. I looked down at the pile of clothes on the chair. I had taken them off, put them on again, and taken them off again already tonight. I did not feel like putting them on once more. I took my mac from the back of the door and put it on over my pyjamas. I went downstairs and put my wellingtons on again. It was a warm night. What was the point of getting dressed up? I would only have to strip off again at the farm.

I got the car out of the garage. Everybody was asleep. Everybody but me. I was just about to start work again. Why the hell had I ever become a country vet? I must have been crazy to pick a job where you worked a seven day week, and nights as well.

Still, things could be worse, I told myself. At least the farm I was going to had electric light. And I could not be all that tired. Not at the age of twenty-four, and in the best of health. Hard work would not kill me – yet.

I was right about Dixon's farm. As I laid out my ropes and instruments in the loose-box I was very thankful that it was well-lit.

I looked at the mare. She was straining hard to give birth to her foal, but in vain, it seemed. There was no sign of any part of the foal. It must be in a bad position.

Still thinking hard I took off my mac. There was a shout of laughter from the farmer. I looked down at my pale blue striped pyjamas. I told him that I had not bothered to dress.

'Oh, I see now,' he said. 'I'm sorry, but I thought I'd got the wrong chap for a second. I saw a bloke just like you at Blackpool last year. Same suit, but he had a top hat, too, and a stick. Did a very good little dance.'

'Can't manage that, I'm afraid,' I said. 'I'm just not in the mood right now.'

I stripped off. The mare trembled as I felt my way inside her. Nothing, nothing, then just a little tail. The foal was in a breech position: that is, not head first as in a normal birth, but upside down. A tricky job in a mare because of the length of the foal's legs.

I sweated and panted for half an hour with ropes and a blunt hook to bring the first leg round. The second leg came more easily. Then the mare gave a great push and the foal shot out on to the straw. To my joy I saw the small body move. When I was working it had not moved, and I thought it was dead. But it was very much alive.

When I had finished drying myself I turned to see the farmer holding out my jacket like a servant.

'Allow me, sir,' he said, and I laughed.

'OK, OK, I'll get dressed next time,' I said. As I was putting my things in the car boot the farmer threw a parcel on the back seat.

'Bit of butter for you,' he said. 'I think a lot of that mare. I've been wanting a foal of hers. Thank you, lad, thank you very much.'

He waved as I moved away. I was pleased that the foal had been alive after all. There is something very sad about the birth of a dead animal.

37 If only they could talk

It was an afternoon when the sun was blazing. I filled my car with Siegfried's dogs. I drove to where an old path ran up the side of a valley. We walked a mile or two on the smooth grass. Then we went straight up the hill-side, to the very top. You could see nearly all the dale laid out beneath.

I was sitting on the grass with the dogs, smelling the sweet breeze. It had met me when I had got off the bus at Darrowby a year ago. I had finished my first year in the job.

I could see many of the farms I had worked on from where I sat. Down there were people who thought I was a pretty fair vet. Some of them thought I was a fool. A few of them were sure I was a genius. One or two of them would set their dogs on me if I set foot inside their gates.

All this in a year. And what about the animals I had got to know? It is a pity that they cannot talk. I should like to know what they think. What do they think of their lives? What do they think of us? Do they manage to get a laugh out of it all?